KINGDOM PEOPLE

Rev David Bown

Illustrated by Teresa Moon

McKnight & Bishop Ltd

Illustrations and cover design by Teresa Moon | www.teresamoon.co.uk

ISBN 978-1-905691-61-6
A CIP catalogue record for this book is available from the British Library

First published in 2019 by McKnight & Bishop Inspire, an imprint of:

McKnight & Bishop Ltd. | 26 Walworth Crescent, Darlington, DL3 0TX
http://www.mcknightbishop.com | info@mcknightbishop.com

This book has been typeset in Garamond-Normal, Bodoni MT & Gill Sans MT,
Printed and bound in Great Britain by Cloc Ltd

About the Publisher

McKnight & Bishop are always on the look-out for new authors and ideas for new books. If you write or if you have an idea for a book, please e-mail us at:

info@mcknightbishop.com

Some things we love are undiscovered authors, open-source software, Creative Commons, crowd-funding, Amazon/Kindle, social networking, faith, laughter and new ideas.

Visit us at www.mcknightbishop.com

*This book is dedicated to
the late Philip Holland,*

*former Methodist Local Preacher
and Head of Theology
at Westminster College.*

CONTENTS

FOREWORD: GOOD NEWS FOR THE WORKING CLASS

Here is a labour of love, a piece of work suffused with a warm enthusiasm, the story of a Methodist minister's fifteen years living and working on one of Europe's biggest housing estates. Methodism has not fared well in its attempts to serve the needs of people living on these sprawling complexes. Nor, indeed, have other Christian churches. That makes this little book all the more remarkable. I've seen the work at first hand and it touched my heart. So when David Bown asked me if I'd write a Preface, there was no hesitation on my part. I just jumped at the chance. Here is gold. What follows, in its simple story-telling way, is a clear announcement of the Kingdom of God for ordinary working class people.

When David arrived at Wythenshawe he found five Methodist churches struggling for survival. Small congregations wilting under a welter of forms to fill, rules to follow, traditions and a whole culture to conform to. It must have been tempting to close most of them and concentrate the membership in one central place. That might have eked things out for a year or two. And our Methodist bigwigs would have been very sympathetic. Such a course of action could easily be presented as a rational way of "managing decline". But David wanted none of that. He set about working with the local people to devise a strategy for the future, a strategy pinned firmly to their understanding of the Kingdom of God. Here was a template that would undergird everything they did. So, with this vision clearly formed, they then went on to evolve a bewildering array of tactical responses to the needs (and opportunities) of the five sets of buildings available to them.

The narrative which follows offers an unusual, an explosive, combination of anecdotal, theoretical and biblical material. This is a cocktail which cannot fail to stir. I laughed out loud at the description of a bus taking a group on an outing which ended up precariously balanced across a hump-backed bridge. I also felt the shock of reading how two units of work went up in flames, victims of an arson attack. The images of ordinary people taking control of their own destiny, one after another is so heart-warming. Health and well-being, culture and the arts, commercial activity and a forum for debate – all find a place in these pulsating centres. Each of them is redesigned to make it fit for a wider purpose. It's truly amazing that the efforts of one person could have triggered so many responses from people of faith, people with questions about life, and committed non-believers alike.

This is an honest account. Difficulties with statutory bodies and ecclesiastic authorities are openly admitted. Failure flirts alongside the undoubted successes of this project. It is so transparent, so honest, filled with such integrity. Here is a proclamation of the Gospel at its most inclusive. "His open arms embrace them all; sinners alone his grace receives."

I feel I must single out the Epilogue for special mention. It describes the plight of people like so many of those who live on the Wythenshawe estate who have been marginalised and side-lined from society over the last decades – people who feel undervalued, unnoticed, ignored. Our churches are as guilty as anyone of feeding this development. It is certainly arguable that people who feel alienated in this way, edged out of the frame, were a key group among those who voted to leave the European Union in the 2016 referendum. Their state of mind is here forensically analysed.

Let me end my contribution to this lovely book by describing the way I became aware of this work being done on the Wythenshawe estate. David Bown invited me to visit him though, he added, he'd quite understand it if someone as important as I (!) didn't have the time to do so. That note did what was intended. It was a red rag to the bull in me and off I went. I arrived late one evening and David took me to a nice restaurant for a meal. I was so overwhelmed by the account he gave of the work, the people, his hopes and his dreams, that I refused to allow him to pay the bill or my travel expenses. And later, I was delighted to find some money to support those undertaking this work. I knew I had found something precious and that it was my privilege to be here where God's work was being done and God's kingdom was being built. Everything I saw the following day confirmed those first impressions and has gone on doing so ever since. My heart was strangely warmed; I left Wythenshawe knowing that I'd been blessed.

Leslie Griffiths.

A COMPULSION TO SHARE
THE KINGDOM OF GOD

I have written this book because it has persistently swirled around in my head and I knew it would continue to until an opportunity was created to share it. It is very rare for a minister to have the chance to begin a new form of Christian ministry and see it through all its pitfalls, to a defining stage that has huge implications. Implications for Christian ministry overall, but on housing estates in particular where a working class culture lives and breathes. Implications, theologically as well as an understanding of the Kingdom of God is understood and lived out; and finally, implications for the Church at large, especially in terms of an individual church's aims and objectives makes it just too important to overlook or disregard.

What I find difficult is constantly using the first person singular, 'I did this', I did that', 'what I saw was' and so on. Difficult because this is not really about me, but I have been told to say what I believe because it is my story and I'm not to be shy in coming forward. It is not about me so much as it is about all of us and by all of us I mean, the whole gambit of people I worked with. Salt of the earth church and estate people, leaders and managers of organisations and individuals, whether or not they occupied formal positions, or whether they knew or knew not they were part of a wider group doing something extremely special.

Forging ahead with a revolutionary form of ministry that offered rich blessing in the multifarious circumstances people and families found them-selves in; is something rewarding in itself. But when individual 'ministries' produce such heart-warming results, someone like me can point out the Christlikeness that is the essential ingredient in that ministry, in that service, in that activity, in that event, in that one-to-one encounter, observation, experience, in situations which turned everything around for good. And such was the Christlikeness that led me time and time again back to the gospels and to the teaching of Jesus. Christ taught about the Kingdom of God from the standpoint of the practical every-day issues that surrounded people of his day and what was to be done about them, in other words the parables. Parables earthed in the all too human nitty-gritty issues that frequently controlled and smothered people, yet told in a way that offered a way out and at the same time pointed to a new society built upon reconciliation, trust and new beginnings.

How could I not write about all this? How could I not stop theologising this – trying to make sense of the parallel situations I saw in Christ's ministry? How could I not stop recognising the significance of the spiritual terms used by the gospel writers and transfer them to our contemporary times? How could I not see the spiritual in people, in individuals, on social occasions and in the complex situations of life and write about it? How could I not truly appreciate one person after another and point out their worth and value, when all they could see of themselves was their own futility and worthlessness? How could I not see all this knowing that Christ saw the same in his day and throughout his ministry and acted upon it? And acted upon it we did with success and delight through the refurbished churches, the innovative and specialised ministries and through keeping everything in check alongside our interpretation of Christ's proclamation about the Kingdom of God.

I had to write it up and make it available to all and sundry so churches especially, but organisations also, can gain something extraordinary from our experience and know-how. Our tried and tested contextual theology of the Kingdom can be a dynamic way into Christian ministry the same as it has been for us, especially when there seems to be a hiatus, an indifferent attitude towards the Kingdom of God as a flight-path for Christian ministry and service. A large proportion of churches seem to favour liturgical services, formal approaches as in baptism and confirmation classes and other mainstream ways to attract people into church, as if that is the primary purpose of being a church. Whereas a simple enquiry concerning Christ's teaching on the Kingdom opens up a myriad expressions of the gospel for any church's every-day ministry, and it is from that powerful source that a highly motivated Christian work of ministry and service can be realized and at the same time, a greater purpose for the church be discovered.

So this book has been written not for me but for and on behalf of everyone involved. It is my hope that the reader may see what we saw, be inspired as we were inspired, be emboldened as we were emboldened and use any ideas that may help reveal a Christ-likeness and establish God's Kingdom as it did for us.

It is more than appropriate at this juncture to acknowledge the invaluable help and guidance given to me by the following: Rev. Charles New, Gwyn Williams, John Berryman, Rev. John Bown, Rev. John Hudson, Margaret Lloyd, Paul Kybird and the late Rev. Dr. William Strawson.

SETTING THE SCENE

The party at my house was in full swing and it was heaving. Over a hundred people came and despite the fact that the garden, with upright piano and celebrity pianist, barbecue and furniture all in place and ready to go, the house became crowded with everyone shuffling around like penguins. That was because just as the party started so did the rain, but that didn't dampen the proceedings, it merely added to the merriment of the occasion. The pianist this time seated at the baby grand, was soon extolling the old favourites in the midst of a continuous flow of 'waiters' bearing eats and drinks above the heads of the throng. And amid the hum of copious conversations; the party was buzzing. These hundred or more guests were a medley, an assemblage of people coming from a wide spectrum of society and yet they all had something special in common.

It was the spirit of commonality that brought them together, a patchwork of trades, skills, ages and abilities. Coming from different backgrounds and experiences of life, they were all activists, and despite the breadth of knowledge and the miscellany of ideology right across the board, they all shared the same commonality of purpose. Instead of just sticking to their own friends and fellow workers, the chatting, laughter and conviviality created a natural interaction; a compelling spark of interest in each other, and their particular contribution to the common good.

I remember at the time, liking it to the story of the Great Banquet in Luke 14:15-24. That was because the food kept running out as more and more people kept coming in. The story in Luke begins when a person notices something different and exclaims: "Blessed is the man who will eat at the feast in the kingdom of God."

On that occasion the original guests invited to the banquet gave feeble excuses for their absence and so the host sent out invitations to a very different clientele: the poor, the blind and people with disabilities, in other words people who were marginalised and discriminated against and not normally invited to such gatherings. Because it was such a large estate with lots of space, the host sent his servant out again and again to find yet more guests and he wasn't disappointed.

The similarity with my party was also the large numbers of guests who kept coming, and despite tumblers and wine glasses all lined up, baked potatoes with different fillings and summer puddings at the ready, the constant flow of guests soon outflanked the food supply. "Go out to the chippy and get as many portions of chips as you can and go to the supermarket for cheese-cake as quickly as you can," said I to my helpers. But no sooner had the extra food arrived that it too was consumed, so I sent them out again this time for pizzas and ice cream. The emergency rations did the trick and not one person who came to the party went away hungry or thirsty.

Although the huge number of guests at my party will have been volunteer workers, managers, service providers, patrons, customers, service users and church people; they were all co-workers, fellow pilgrims, sisters and brothers involved in the work of the Kingdom of God. Not all will have claimed that; some might even have felt shy by such a suggestion. But at the end of the day, that's what it boiled down to because I recognised the value of the work they were doing and the important spiritual contribution they were making. And as the party continued, I thought to myself, "It is good that my house is heaving with people tonight, a meeting of various life journeys, a reflection of God's Kingdom."

The party was as described and took place when the pioneering project work was in full swing. It had developed to a significant and defining stage and its personal stimulus was infectious. So welcome to these pages about the Kingdom of God in Wythenshawe, the people who became part of it, and how it all happened.

HOW IT ALL BEGAN

I t is not every church or every cluster of churches found in a Methodist Circuit any more than it is not in every Christian ministry or even every minister's own experience of his/her every day work; that the Kingdom of God is at the heart of everything that takes place. It is because this was the case among the five Methodist Churches and their ministries at Wythenshawe and became profoundly inspirational, that fuelled the desire to tell all. Consequently, it describes and illustrates the way the Kingdom of God as observed in Christ's own ministry and teaching was used as the foundation, stimulus and guiding principle in the pioneering ministries of all five churches, at the start of new and exciting beginnings.

The setting is a very large housing estate directly south of Manchester city centre called Wythenshawe. Its cultural history and ethos is typical of a society steeped in its working class roots, which by its very nature gave immense stimulus to the grass-roots Kingdom of God enterprises that made such good connections with the indigenous folk. From the outset, and as a Kingdom of God theology and philosophy would suggest, the 'ministries-in-waiting', in other words people orientated activities and services being planned, were intended for all people on the estate regardless of any church connections and especially those whose needs were greatest. This was like throwing the doors of the churches wide open and going where the people were; to their homes, to the children's schools, the shopping centre, health centres, community centres, children centres and not least involvement in the complexities of their personal and family lives, especially where much needed advocacy was required.

Involvement of this scale was only possible due to close working relationships with organisations who became not only partners in Christian ministry, but partners in the sweat and toil of the work of the Kingdom of God itself. The formation of close co-operative and working relationships with service-led organisations was part of the plan from the beginning; and the beginning came in the form of a comprehensive written proposal detailing new ways the churches could play their part, by offering much needed distinctive ministries with pastoral care, to a largely vulnerable people often exploited and persistently neglected. The organisations that entered into partnerships with the churches included those from statutory and charity/trust establishments, besides voluntary and community-led organisations. Some operated Monday to Friday while others worked on a weekly or monthly basis and all of them adopted what was a shared mission initiative, which the churches and organisations all signed up to.

Do you have good powers of imagination because I want you to picture the setting I'm opening up to you? Organisations, groups and individual people, flourishing in their activity-led work which on the one hand are singularly focussed and on the other hand, their individual input becomes like the threads of a spider's web in all its wholeness. And what I'm describing are church people, helpers, a range of volunteers and encouragers more than willing to roll their sleeves up and get stuck in. And stuck in they did, running the charity shop, rummage sales, cafes, alternative therapies, counselling, the gym, computer club and so on; and all to their credit and to the well-being of everyone. I have huge admiration for them including the organisations because as their work and endeavours were much valued, these salt-of-the-earth people were undertaking something of immense practical worth, but with massive spiritual depth which showed me just how valuable they were in themselves. Could they see what I was seeing? Could they appreciate their work as a contribution to something bigger? Could they see God in what they were doing? Could they see an association with what they were hearing about the Kingdom of God? Probably not as clear cut as I would have wished except maybe, through a prevailing ethos, a spiritual atmosphere that was as definitive as it was indistinguishable between all of them and every activity.

In the hope of establishing more clearly the picture of the five Wythenshawe churches, here is a good starting point. The five churches are:

- Baguley Hall with their project name of: 'The Harvest Centre'

- Brownley Green and project name of: 'Brownley Green Village'

- Lawton Moor and their project name 'New Dawn Association'

- Northenden with: 'Northenden Community Projects'

- St. Andrew's and project:'New Horizons'

All five churches with their projects had mission statements describing the specialist nature of their enterprises and those statements feature in the chapter that illustrates their work and working relationships. Important as every person was in the overall scheme of things, those with a distinctive role were the project managers. Each project manager oversaw all their church's project work including very important liaison with managers and leaders of the different projects. Their role cannot be overstated as they held in balance church aspirations alongside that of all the project work. This required excellent PR ability to encourage and offer help and guidance especially in the submission of funding applications, appreciating all the preparatory work funding applications required.

It is not appropriate to single out individual project managers any more than it is from the vast pool of human resources as a whole, but when consideration is given to the breadth of an individual's commitment to other areas of professional voluntary work and interests, their overall contribution to and participation in the work of the Kingdom of God, is overwhelmingly second to none. It is also the case and unsurprisingly, that a project manager is more than likely to hold the brief for other church responsibilities and not least among them is the maintenance of the church's property. Where this was the case and appreciating such commitment would have been continuous over that person's life-time; not only me, the church and the projects but the Kingdom of God itself will have been hugely privileged to be in receipt of such dedication and faithfulness.

All this means I cannot but acknowledge and pay huge respect to the true vocational spirit and worth so selflessly given; and vocation it is in all the depth of its meaning and personal sacrifice.

So what I am introducing you to and will illustrate as you read further into this discourse, is a variety of activities associated with each church, portraits of people with an unmistakeable Christlikeness, churches that knocked down their internal walls and refurbished their premises to accommodate specialised services, stories and events which in themselves were modern day parables, achievements in bringing individuals together usually not seen anywhere near a church, community events of holistic aspiration and enterprises which were as prophetic as they were of therapeutic value.

The end result was a reversal to the expected closure of the churches and, instead, all five of them embarked upon new beginnings using the principles and values of the Kingdom of God as their starting point represented in Christ's work and teaching.

At the heart of my thesis is the revelation of the Incarnate God in the personalities, community settings and project work that are identified as being the work of the Kingdom of God. I have simply sought to express this revelation through the practical aspects of the ministerial work I have experienced and perceived, through insights given me in my understanding of a theology of the Kingdom of God. Use of the title 'Incarnate God' is important because as well as being the work of God, the entire project-driven programme, earthed as it was in Christ's teachings, enabled the enterprises to acquire a spiritual depth and quality that was unmistakeably associated with the Incarnate God himself. Another way of expressing this is by saying God was there working with us, in us, through us, around us, and God was there because of us; and the reference 'us' is used inclusively to involve also recipients and patrons of our services and individuals passing through. Indeed, it is a central claim of my thesis that God is frequently perceived not least through the ordinary individual and sometimes to great effect.

Using Christ's teachings on the Kingdom of God as the foundation upon which all future ministry and church work was to proceed, gave the whole operation a theological and spiritual frame-work from which an affinity with the person of Christ and his teaching became highly significant. Such a template in theory and in practice meant the whole vision became a highly successful reality and at the same time, personal and community aspects of social and spiritual renewal became real to hordes of people in diverse ways. A distinctive spiritual 'presence' with incarnational overtones became noticeable in many areas of community life, in working relationships as they developed and in its overall contribution to social and spiritual regeneration. I have sought to the best of my ability in the chapters of this book to 'open up' this particular appreciation of the spiritual and the incarnational within our midst, whilst at the same time accepting it is not necessarily a common or chosen theological approach by many of my fellow ministers, church leaders or churches these days. This of course does not make it an easy quest to elucidate satisfactorily my theological and spiritual discoveries, especially in the knowledge that other churches have their own and different priorities of church work and ministry, which in many instances are dissimilar from this 'Wythenshawe' approach. Evidence of this and the aforesaid assertion is partly illustrated in chapter 1 under the heading 'Wythenshawe Churches 1998'. Suffice to say it is my hope that these insights borne out of Christ inspired grass roots every-day practical ministry, will add to an on-going deliberation on best practice for contemporary Christian ministry.

I have purposely chosen not to write chronologically because I didn't want to mislead. While it is true, all five churches operated from the same hymn sheet and shared identical aspirations, their ministries and overall experiences were unique to themselves. That doesn't mean there was not common ground between them, there was and lots of it and for that reason I chose not to list each church's work in a repetitive and customary way. Similarly in the use of biblical texts and passages; they too are purposely not presented in list form, so that commentary can be directed to the singular situations the texts identified. This is not dissimilar to the way the gospel writers wrote, as their style depicted every-day life. Likewise, a greater significance is discovered in the title 'Kingdom of God' when it is appreciated within the particular context for which it was used.

Before delving into the main subject matter of the book and going headlong through the chapters, I want to draw attention to some headline titles. These titles and their commentaries will be helpful preparation especially when considering the person of Christ, his character and status; and that compelling title he uses over and over again: 'The Kingdom of God'.

CHRISTLIKENESS AND THE INCARNATE GOD

In the early days of our developing work during the first three or so years, we used a text from the Magnificat as a mentor, encourager, as a guiding light: "He has brought down rulers from their thrones but has lifted up the humble. He has filled the hungry with good things but has sent the rich away empty." (Luke 1:52-53). The prophetic nature of that text in relation to the people we were serving with all their complex social issues, spoke eloquently about Christ as the Incarnate God but not just as someone who lived two thousand years ago, but as a divine presence very much in the here and now. One or two of our people thought the use of that text from the Magnificat could seem a bit patronising and not entirely appropriate, but not so the text's prophetic message coming as it did from the voice of a pregnant Mary declaring that her expectant child will not only be the defender and saviour of the humble and poor, but more importantly, he will be God personified in the person of Jesus. This means of course that the Jesus who spoke fluently about the Kingdom of God alongside his own versatile ministry and one-to-one encounters, was at the same time none other than God in human form dwelling in the midst of the people.

This brings us to Jesus the Incarnate God and to people's Christ-likeness being a revelation of God. Such a revelation is a statement about the Incarnate God who continues to dwell among humanity through those who, known or unknown to themselves, becomes as Christ to their fellow human beings. That is the overarching theme running through this thesis and particular consideration of it is explored in the story about the Rummage and Christ's statement in the parable of the Sheep and the Goats: "Truly, I say to you, as you did it to one of the least of these my brethren, you did it to me." (Matthew 25:40). This is explored in chapter 4 under the heading: 'The Rummage'.

Examples of individual people whose stories and testimonies reveal a Christ-likeness has featured in the characters that I have portrayed and in the situations that surrounded them. A Christ-likeness is not confined to a particular person any more than it is confined to the work they might do, but the likeness is noticeable or discernible in the characters they are and in the sensitivities they reveal. Some are highlighted in these pages as unforgettable portraits, but there are others who in their own way also showed the hallmarks of the unseen Christ. What is of fascination and interest is the way such a presence is perceived and it is not unusual to spot it in what the world might consider to be a very ordinary unassuming person, whose generous spirit, or endearing sensitivity, loyalty and love, compassion, kindness and all manner of spiritual virtues, simply stand out and stand alongside some of the individuals Christ himself gave significance to.

Just as Christ's entry into the world could, with qualification, be said to have been couched in simplicity and humility. It is noteworthy that the majority of examples of Christ-likeness that feature in Christ's ministry are likewise characters revealing a similar simplicity and humility. Perhaps due to a focus of attention being elsewhere concerning the divine presence, it can be the case it is simply not expected to be encountered in contemporary society, but that is not the claim of this thesis. Indeed, it might give credence to the following text in the prologue of John's gospel: "He came to that which was his own, but his own did not receive him." (John1:11). The point is, as is verified in these chapters, that a God-given Christ-likeness has been our reality and experienced among a cross-section of individuals, the privilege of which has been to the advantage of us all.

CHRIST'S PRINCIPLES

One way of understanding these principles is by appreciating the examples given in his teaching from the passages known as 'The Sermon on the Mount' (Matthew 5:1 - 7:28) which consist of the following affirmations:

- Live according to righteous behaviour & values
- Be an example
- Live honestly in everything
- Hold no grievances
- Sort out disputes
- Recognise when dishonesty looms & take diversionary action
- Avoid tainting others with your own imperfections
- Be straightforward with the truth
- Give at a cost willingly
- Love even enemies
- Give to others secretly
- Do everything sincerely without wanting recognition
- Do your piety in secret
- Keep personal possessions away from a false importance
- Be free of worry & trust basic needs will be met
- Refrain from bigotry & intolerance
- Do good and good will be returned
- Keep on your path of integrity & do not be distracted away from it
- Do not be taken in by empty promises
- Build every value on a strong foundation

A similar exercise can be done with the nine Beatitudes in Matthew 5: 1-12. The circumstance or situation the beatitude's portrays reveals an exceptional human quality which is followed with an equally prophetic declaration because of the quality thus shown. It is as though each attribute is a segment of what can be described as Christ's principles. Another source of information through teaching that does the same thing is the parables. There are 46 parables ascribed to Jesus. Each one is a short story that teaches a moral or spiritual truth by analogy or similarity. They featured something from everyday life that could be easily understood. They were cleverly composed and designed to gain maximum interest and create maximum impact in order to impart Christ's new teaching and get people to think and behave to a new social and ethical order. As well as offering guiding principles in themselves, they demonstrate the standard by which Christ lived his own life, the values of which are the key attributes of his teaching. Hence the truths elicited through his parabolic teaching are the principles he himself believed in and lived by.

In consideration of Christ's aims and objectives, it is helpful to appreciate what is meant by aims and objectives in relation to proposals and enterprises the like of which Christ had embarked upon.

CHRIST'S AIMS & OBJECTIVES

An aim is a long-term goal or an achievable vision, a task or piece of work that needs to be accomplished. In relation to Christ's aims, these are set out in a variety of ways in biblical texts the most familiar and interesting ones being the Old Testament prophets including: Isaiah as in chapter 11 where the future messiah is seen to judge with righteousness and respond to the poor with justice. In chapter 35 the prophet paints a futuristic scene of idyllic serenity and harmony. In chapter 53 the future Messiah is pictured as the Suffering Servant and in chapter 61 the aims appertaining to Christ's future work are the texts he chose to read in the synagogue and announced to his hearers that in Him they are fulfilled. There are similar prophecies in the New Testament that illustrate in dramatic form the aims associated with Christ's future work and not least by his own mother in Luke 1: 46-55 the Song of Mary known as the Magnificat; also 1: 67-79 The Song of Zechariah known as the Benedictus; The Beatitudes in Matthew 5: 3-11 and Christ's proclamation as already mentioned in Luke 4: 18-19. These and other statements reveal Christ's aims that he set out to achieve through his work of preaching and teaching, healing and blessing, personal example and through his sacrificial love.

One of the clearest examples of Christ's aims is given in Matthew 4: 23-25. It is at the outset of his ministry and through describing what Jesus began doing, the author of the gospel gives a pro-active picture of Jesus healing people and speaks of 'preaching the good news of the Kingdom'. To quote: "Jesus went throughout Galilee, teaching in their synagogues, preaching the good news of the Kingdom, and healing every disease and sickness among the people. News about him spread all over Syria, and people brought to him all who were ill with various diseases, those suffering severe pain, the demon-possessed, those having seizures, and the paralysed, and he healed them. Large crowds from Galilee, the Decapolis, Jerusalem, Judea and the region across the Jordan followed him." This establishes that Christ's aims were to teach, to preach and to heal; and it became clear further into Christ's ministry that these characteristics plus others that featured in his on-going work, all found their origin in what became known as 'the good news of the Kingdom', 'Kingdom' being the operative word. This means Christ's aims were embedded in the work of the Kingdom, a work and a Kingdom that this thesis epitomises and thoroughly explores in the chapters that follow.

Objectives encapsulate specific steps or intended to be taken to achieve the aims or the exercise or mission. In Christ's case his objectives were fulfilled through the way he conducted every aspect of his personal life and that of his ministry. The subjects he chose to use as parables; his answers to a multiplicity of questions; the way he taught and gave leadership through complex circumstances; new insights given to long held customs and traditions; and objectives revealed through his healing work, miracles he performed and not least through his teaching on the Kingdom of God.

From these principles exercised by Christ, his aims and objectives deduced from his teaching and the values he held dear, Christianity developed a moral and ethical order that society could embrace and through which it could conduct its affairs. Kingdom values are the guiding criterion that express and give meaning to behaviour and action especially when it shows respect and honours the true worth 'integrity' of creation, among which are individuals, communities and whole nations. Kingdom values are catalogued in myriad descriptive ways by the gospel writers and through our interpretation of them. To capture something of their arresting manner, let us conduct a simple exercise by looking at one such example: The Parable of the Great Banquet (Luke 14:15-24).

Jesus told this highly dramatic story in response to an amazing exclamation by someone who was most likely a Jew and could have been a Pharisee. His sudden and excitable interjection reveals a person of learned standing and someone who showed much interest in Jesus and was even prepared to think for him-self and to think in a prophetic way. He was animated by the events as they unfolded around the meal table. The suspicious host and his guests were already in critical watching mode and Jesus zoomed in unabashed in the questions he asked and the healing he ministered to a man suffering from dropsy. Further questions Jesus asked his fellow guests about social morality drew no response, so he suggested turning on its head the long-held convention of always honouring the most noble with the most grandiose status; in other words reversing completely the priorities that governed the social order. Lastly, Jesus suggests a radical alternative guest-list for a dinner party! It appears that these 'outrageous' recommendations positively inspired his fellow guest, hence his animated outburst: "Blessed is the man who will eat at the feast of the Kingdom of God." (Luke 14:15). Jesus then goes on to reinforce all he had just said and done by telling the story that has become known as the Great Banquet.

We can deduce from this the way Jesus held fast to his principles whilst not showing disrespect to those whose own principles were objectionable to him, but at the same time spared no effort in questioning his hearers about their perverse sense of justice, code of ethics and personal morality. Jesus lived according to his principles of fairness, equality, respect, consideration and generosity. His principles did not isolate him from his critics and neither did they distance him from engaging with his critics; on the occasions that did happen, it was because of the negativity of his critics and the principles they held. It is interesting that the values drawn from Christ's principles are not dissimilar from the list the Apostle Paul gives as being 'fruits of the Spirit' (Galatians 5:22). These consist of love, joy, peace, patience, kindness, goodness, faithfulness, gentleness and self-control. To these can be added others including: forgiveness, integrity, self-less-ness, empathy, identity, understanding, courage; besides many more.

In the same way that Christ's principles and values were his bedrock, likewise the principles and values drawn from our knowledge of the Kingdom of God became for the churches and their partner organisations, the foundation upon which everything else proceeded.

KINGDOM OF GOD AS A TEMPLATE

The Oxford Advanced Learner's Dictionary defines 'template' as something that serves as a model for others to copy. I am unclear and unknowing what future the five churches could have expected from the beginning of our pilgrimage in early 1999, if we had not used the Kingdom of God as our template. What I do know is that if we had relied solely on the old tried and tested forms of church ministry and pursued them exclusively as churches on our own, we not only would have achieved very little, but we would have negated our duties and responsibilities to people too often left on the side-lines of society, given our church communities and buildings only a short-term future; and we would have impoverished ourselves from living to the full the good news of the Kingdom.

Matthew recalls the dynamics of Christ's ministry when he says: "Jesus went through all the towns and villages, teaching in their synagogues, preaching the good news of the Kingdom and healing every disease and sickness. When he saw the crowds he had compassion on them, because they were harassed and helpless, like sheep without a shepherd. Then he said to his disciples, the harvest is plentiful but the workers are few. Ask the Lord of the harvest, therefore, to send out workers into his harvest field." (Matthew 9:35-38)

The Kingdom of which Jesus gave voice to in innumerable ways, fulfilled in practical and innovative ways; and manifested dramatically with much emotion and empathy, became our template. It was a template that was not our exclusive possession, but a universal template that spelt out clearly what inclusivity really means in the context of God's Kingdom. It means that all people, irrespective of religious tradition, prevailing culture, class, circumstance, their background, country of origin, their place or non-place in society or their local community; it means absolutely all people. This was something we took to heart and made sure it was and remained the bedrock of our understanding and appreciation of the people we were not only called to serve, but to acknowledge as co-inheritors of the Kingdom, as our sisters and brothers.

The biblical text from Matthew gives clear evidence not only about those who occupy the Kingdom, but details the work of the Kingdom by giving significance to Christ's ministry of teaching, preaching and healing, which is precisely what our churches, our project work and our miscellaneous services were delivering in their diverse ways. Because of the work's diverse nature and application by church and non-church organisations alike, it was necessary to look purposefully at the benevolence and services being given, to identify it as work of the Kingdom and to see the theological and spiritual connotations; especially when it was work by our professional service-led organisations involved in health and welfare. But it was there in the midst of all our work by the smallest organisation, the one-person operation or by personal example even if unknown by the benefactor; and in whatever ways we engaged with, or related to, anyone and everyone; it was unmistakeably there.

Another detail elucidated in the Matthew passage is its message about the state of Israel. Jesus said that they (meaning Israel) are 'like sheep without a shepherd' and then came this statement directed to his disciples: "The harvest is plentiful but the workers are few. Ask the Lord of the harvest, to send out workers into his harvest field." The 'workers' are those who are agents of the Kingdom who would lead people into or embrace people within the Kingdom. And when that happens, it would be like a harvest when all the crops are gathered into a safe place, only in this instance Jesus is talking about people who in one way or another are blessed with God's grace. The task Jesus was asking his disciples to undertake was to pray to God that 'workers' would indeed come and lead people into, or embrace them with the Kingdom of God. It is my conviction and it is the heart of this thesis, that such 'agents' as I have called them, in other words, the church and non-church partners engaged in this great work of social and spiritual regeneration, were those 'workers' who I perceived being in a very real and practical way, the unseen Christ.

An appreciation and acknowledgement of such a divine truth makes the Kingdom of God when used as a template, not only the right course of action by the Church, but such affiliation with Christ and his diverse ministry extends the concept of incarnation (Christlikeness) to new levels of understanding. It also more than suggests that the Kingdom of God as a foundation for the work of God by churches or by other means, was absolutely right for the Wythenshawe churches as it can be or should be, by all like-minded 'agents' of God's Kingdom.

THE KINGDOM OF GOD FOR EVERYONE

An appreciation of the title 'Kingdom of God' or 'Kingdom of Heaven' is both essential for the purposes of this thesis and for an understanding of its profundity. David Field writing in the Lion Handbook of the Bible reveals the extraordinary diversity that underpins the numerous ways the term 'Kingdom of God' is used by Jesus. This shows its appeal and value to literally everyone, to the Jew, to the Gentile, to the outcast and to the non-religious people; and it shows also its own unique character in the diverse circumstances where it is applied and the message in those situations it conveys.

David Field highlights the important part the Kingdom of God exercised in Christ's teaching, and throughout his ministry. He points out that Jews would not wish even to say the name 'God' because God is too sacred to speak his name, which is why Matthew as a Jew and writing primarily to the Jewish people uses the title: Kingdom of Heaven; unlike Mark and Luke who use Kingdom of God. Such is its importance, it is not surprising the title first appears at the beginning of Christ's work of ministry and teaching; "The time has come" Jesus announces, "The Kingdom of God is near. Repent and believe the Good News." What follows, is an amazing articulation and interpretation with countless presentations by Jesus of the Kingdom of God's universality, in that it was unmistakeably present in everything associated with him.

The Jews had long waited for the coming Kingdom which is why in Mark's gospel it speaks about Joseph of Arimathaea as "waiting for the Kingdom of God" (Mark 15:43), but the Jews were anticipating, when finally the kingdom would be inaugurated, an entirely different Kingdom from the one announced and established by Jesus. The twist being, the Kingdom in fact was in their midst, it was in the very person of Christ himself yet they remained looking elsewhere in tandem with their continual 'waiting' and 'expectancy' as they had done for centuries. It is the three gospels of Mark, Luke and Matthew that uninhibitedly declare that in Jesus the Kingdom of God has become a living reality.

Visible signs of the Kingdom over and above those witnessed in the person of Jesus himself became hugely significant, he tells the disciples of John the Baptist, "Go back and report to John what you hear and see: The blind receive sight, the lame walk, those who have leprosy are cured, the deaf hear, the dead are raised, and the good news is preached to the poor." (Matthew 11:4-5). Those signs of the Kingdom are aligned to Christ's ministry; other signs are those elucidated in his teaching and these include: parables, sermons and sayings, conversations with individuals and people not least his disciples and through his own life-style and the principles he lived by.

Throughout my writing I allude to the principles and values of the Kingdom of God because everything associated with our work found its meaning and purpose in those values; values which became the heart and soul of all our work. It is important therefore to appreciate what is meant by Kingdom of God principles and their values. Principles in relation to the 'Kingdom of God' are the aims and objectives that governed Christ's own ministry, directed his teaching and what is discernible from his personal life-style and relationships. That Jesus was a person of great principle is unquestioned and his principles were what he believed, what he taught, the fundamental standards he set himself and the code of practice he lived by.

If I am honest with myself, I have to admit to being uncomfortable about those Christian community and church congregations that give the appearance of being exclusive fraternities; and to be honest for the second time, whether it is the intention of churches or not, exclusivity is the message that is generally conveyed. That impression of being set apart as a people is not altogether surprising for the following reasons:

The challenging message of many churches is for people to change their ways and become followers of Christ and join congregations of similar like-minded people; and within those gatherings and assemblies, friendships of depth and quality, besides meetings for mutual fellowship, strengthen that strong feeling of togetherness, especially when it is accompanied with a shared acknowledgement of what Christ means corporately. Add to that strong sense of solidarity, a distinct common purpose to live the Christian life and evangelise; and the intention that more people will discover a common entity and therefore embrace an unmistakeable church culture is what happens. Whichever way it is viewed, the end result spells out an exclusive community.

Another way churches can become restrictive if not exclusive communities is through their system of membership and the access it gives to be an active volunteer in the name of the church, but denied to those who are not official members. It goes without saying that if you are a signed up member of a club it puts you in a different position from someone who is not a member especially in the exercising of responsibilities or duties in the name of the club. Likewise with church membership, it can be a necessary and even a legal requirement for a host of administrative reasons as well as keeping everything neat, tidy and up to date on an organisational level. Being an actual member can convey what is to some people an important emotional feeling, that they do truly belong and are not 'outside' the community or assembly of gathered people; and that can be a critical factor for good, but such a system can seriously be viewed as a form of privilege conferred on the select and not on everyone.

Regardless of the whys and wherefores of church membership, by virtue of the system within which it operates, it generates an exclusive community. By so doing, an anomaly is created that is counter to the message and relationship offered by Christ in his teaching on the Kingdom of God, and especially through his demonstrative work of that God-given Kingdom.

One of the big features that stands' out through our Wythenshawe work and relationships is the acknowledgement that all people are equal; of equal worth, of equal importance and of equal value. With that acknowledgement, there was not any differentiation between people of all ages, different backgrounds, circumstances or abilities with whom the churches, partner organisations and the projects had contact or association. All the individual communities were part of the one combined Wythenshawe community represented as they were through their involvement and participation in the Kingdom of God; and appreciated especially by the churches as the one family of God.

Wythenshawe Oasis as a charity in its own right was at the heart of the work of the Kingdom as were the partner organisations and all the maintenance and administrative personnel. It is when they are placed together or seen as one big operational working party, that the vocational aspect of the enterprises and sheer dedication to the cause became the uniting factor around which was a strong spirituality and a spiritual quality that permeated through our relationships and enhanced our work.

It goes without saying that it is my hope and wish that as many ordinary church people and non-church people as possible will read these pages and gain interest and insights from them; as there is also optimism that the readership will include ministers in training, church leaders, as well as service providers and clergy and pastors already on the job. It is more than appropriate to mention those who have given help and encouragement in the writing of these pages and that is best achieved by citing those to whom this book owes its existence and they are the lovely people of Wythenshawe; the ones that are directly involved in church work and worship and the ones who have been involved in the work of the Kingdom in other ways. Together they form a very large and dynamic family of God to whom I cannot pay enough tribute except by devoting this book to them in appreciation for the timeless encouragement they have given to me. Unknown to them, for such is their humility and seeming 'unnoticeable-ness', yet it is precisely they through their Christlikeness and in their sometimes all-too human issues that surround them, that have taught me most about the Incarnate God and his Kingdom on earth. Thank you to all of you who count me your friend, to those of you with whom I worked, to the managers of organisations whose colleagueship I have valued immensely, to partner organisations large and small and to those of you far and near whose interest in us never dimmed and whose support kept us going.

CHAPTER 1:
THE KINGDOM OF GOD AS THE FOUNDATION FOR EVERYONE

T his chapter sets the scene and introduces the wonderful housing estate of Wythenshawe and the five Wythenshawe Methodist Churches before going on to explore in cultural terms, relationships by church and people and relationships by Christ and the people of his day.

INTRODUCING WYTHENSHAWE

Welcome to Wythenshawe, to a mixed society, an international society and to it "all happens here" society. One of the largest housing estates in Europe covering an area of 11 square miles on the south side of Manchester bordering Cheshire; Wythenshawe is Manchester's largest district, a massive housing estate that was started in the 1920s intended as a 'garden city' where an overspill population could be rehoused away from the slums and squalor of industrial Manchester.

By 1939 the population was 40,000 and the average working wage was £3 a week and house rent which was only just affordable would have been between 65p and 75p. After an interruption in house building due to the Second World War, housing stock and amenities began to flourish again from the middle 1940s onwards. Shops, community facilities and employment followed on belatedly and, through higher density housing that was built during the 1950s, the population grew to 100,000. The shopping centre was finished in the 1960s and Wythenshawe Forum incorporating leisure centre with a swimming pool, cafe, library, theatre and

From small beginnings

meeting rooms was finally opened in 1971. Development of the estate's infrastructure continued through the 1970s and 1980s; and by the end of the 1990s most of it was in place. Between 1999 and 2002 the shopping centre was substantially renovated and that hailed a ten year period of huge investment and substantial change.

Cloistered between two sections of the estate is Wythenshawe Park, a large grassed area surrounded by old established trees with paths and tracks criss-crossing the park connecting different areas of Wythenshawe. The park boasts many amenities including football pitches, tennis courts, bowling greens, an athletics track, riding stables, a horticultural centre, children's play areas and a community farm. There are also 12 'domestic style' parks and 18 woodland areas strategically situated on the estate.

Most notable among the changes the investment brought has been a combination of new amenities including 3 Primary Schools, 5 Academies, 2 Health Centres incorporating walk-in clinics, 5 Sure Start children centres, 3 leisure centres including the complex at the Forum with its gymnasium, an Adult Education college, a residential complex for long-term and respite care and a Police Station. Some of these new institutions have replaced former buildings, whilst others have been part of an amalgamation process. The Forum development alone was a sizeable investment in social cohesion by making provision for a re-furbished library, a learning centre, nursery, café, as well health facilities and the leisure activities already mentioned. The location also doubles up as a meeting place for exhibitions, stalls and occasional promotional and celebratory events. During this time the council housing stock owned and administered by Manchester City Council was transferred to two housing associations which in turn entered into a comprehensive programme of up-grading all their dwellings the total of which in 2013 stood at 14,000 homes.

At the same time, industrial and commercial units and their respective businesses, which are substantial, have also gone through transformations involving new developments and industries whilst some major long-term enterprises have upped-sticks and moved away. As part of an on-going re-development, the shopping centre also known locally as the civic centre or town centre, has gone through yet more transformations attracting retailers with high street brands at a loss to its own traditional market with their universally renowned stalls. But by far the newest acquisition to life in Wythenshawe has been the installation of the new Metrolink. This tram system, that began services on the estate in 2014, makes connections with other major towns and places in Greater Manchester besides the direct line through Wythenshawe to Manchester Airport and Wythenshawe Hospital. However, special recognition must be given to the airport and the hospital and singled out because of the appreciable expansion of both those establishments and not least to the benefit of Wythenshawe people and residents. Easy access to the M60 and the M56 means Wythenshawe is a hub to a vast commercial and industrial network of corporations with access to surrounding conurbations.

As has been observed, a movement of change in Wythenshawe occurred during the fifteen years between 1998 and 2013 in particular and part of those changes, especially in the latter years, is noticeable in the growth of private housing. With the right, by the sitting tenant, to buy their council house together with an increasing development of private sector housing on the estate, the parity between 'tenants' and 'home owners' has shifted in recent years and continues to do so. Despite tenants being no longer able to buy their homes as in the past, the disparity between the two could mean a change in the prevailing 'estate culture'.

Statistical data reveals that half the housing (50%) in 2011 was privately owned. Two facts emerge from this. The social mix of people in Wythenshawe is becoming more and more diverse and at the same time, new housing being built is predominantly for the private market. After a dip in the overall population from 100,000 in the 1950s to 66,000 in 2001, due in part by succeeding generations of family members not being allowed to inherit their parents' tenancies, by 2011 the population had grown again to 72,000. 1,500 businesses catering for more than 52,000 jobs, another indicator of the density and volume of working people resident on the estate. By far the two largest employers are Manchester Airport with 20,000 employees and Wythenshawe Hospital employing 5,000 people; and 7,000 visitors a day are said to patronise the civic centre with an average of 15,000 popping into the library every month.

It became clear from all the changes that had taken place and the ever new and different changes that were on-going, that the five Methodist churches, came to an understanding in terms of what these changes would mean to them and how those changes would need to influence their theology of mission; in other words spell out what the churches' place and purpose was to be. Results of an extensive survey published in January 1999 clearly set the agenda for such a mission initiative and pivotal was a plethora of ministries that would be 'service-led'. Steering the thinking and planning behind this was the needs of the people and in particular, those services which in fact were being denied the people because they were quite simply unaffordable. Consequently some of the most acute needs among a large proportion of people from all over the estate were not being met and neither were there signs that one day they would be. These and other 'to be addressed' observations that preoccupied most consideration from the survey were as follows:

- Poor health
- Low education attainment
- Low self-esteem
- People with learning difficulties
- Loneliness
- Lack of motivation
- Unemployment
- Personal isolation
- Personal & family problems
- Debt & money issues
- Poor diet
- Lacking an awareness of a person's own potential and its possibilities

All of these concerns and issues could too easily be misunderstood, misplaced and wrongly addressed by churches and institutions but for one major consideration, a true acknowledgement of Wythenshawe's prevailing working class background, ethos and culture. Such a culture is distinctive in these ways; it is down to earth, has its own set of values, attitudes, morality, behaviour, 'vocabulary' and life-style. If the people's needs were in any way going to be addressed, they would need to be addressed within the prevailing culture not outside of it. Organisations and institutions including the church fail over and over again when they knowingly or unwittingly create a space or a distance between themselves and the other person because of the difference between their cultures. Without a sensitivity to this and appropriate ways to address it, personnel and organisations from the service sector without a working class empathy or identity can very easily appear aloof and patronizing, or misunderstand situations as much as they are misunderstood, because they are not on the same wave-length as the people. Neither it is the case, that the people from Wythenshawe should be expected to appreciate and incorporate some of the finesse of the 'other' (middle class) culture into their own. That would be degrading and unappreciative of that important sense of equality which should be undisputable. This is the salient point when working among people and communities of a working class culture. An appreciation and desire to embrace the culture is an essential ingredient by professional and volunteer workers, organisations and establishments across the board.

And speaking of things cultural and the ever on-going changes that occur which adds to the 'spirit' of the place, enter now the international dimension. The new residents from countries representing the four corners of the world must rank as one of the biggest changes Wythenshawe has ever experienced. Originally an all-white British populace, Wythenshawe can easily boast these days being an estate diverse in ethnicity, colourful in cultural expression, rich in worldwide consciousness and vibrant in its social integration. The international community began to find their home in Wythenshawe from 2005. Some came on visas to work there, some to study and attend higher education, some as migrants, some as refugees and others as asylum seekers. One of the overall contributions their presence has made can best be illustrated in the success of the wonderful international celebrations arranged and organised by the re-generation team at Wythenshawe. It is in the flare and glow of the national costumes, the music, the dancing, the food, the decorations and the sheer friendliness of the occasions that has given the estate that extra ingredient and made the place global. It is an asset not to be underestimated and one from which all people can glean something good and positive, as well as making a contribution to harmonious relations and community togetherness.

So, the housing estate of Wythenshawe is in fact 11 square miles in circumference within which are 70,000 - 80,000 plus people. There are several major through roads and some minor roads that criss-cross the estate, from which there are numerous very narrow cul-de-sacs; narrow because there were few privately owned cars in the 1930s and 40s so little or no car parking was required at the time when plans of the estate were drawn up and the roads first built.

Yes, there are some hideous deadly goings on among gangs and some individuals are part of a network at war with themselves, but they are a very small minority. It's true that there are also those who sponge off others and not least from the

State and will fiddle their way into getting State benefits they are not entitled to. There are even those who make life hell for their neighbours and a never ending stream of people who are exploited over and over again. Not to mention the under-class, families and residents not able to manage on their own and those struggling without a safe refuge while having to cope with all manner of learning difficulties and disadvantages.

But forget not and by-pass not the vast majority of Wythenshawe people who are fantastic in every way and, given the opportunity, excel in their common identity, play their part in community cohesion, contribute tirelessly through their generous spirit and are a credit to themselves and everything they stand for.

WYTHENSHAWE CHURCHES 1998

There was a reason why the five Wythenshawe Methodist Churches were characterised as being in 'special measures' - well that's the current terminology for failing schools and other institutions, but it equally applies to the situation facing the Methodist Church in relation to Wythenshawe. And the short answer to the question why they were so near to closure is because all five churches had their heydays long ago and had been in constant decline for decades. A longer answer would need a detailed exploration into the methodology and approach of the Methodist Church to churches on a working class estate, in terms of their living, working and breathing a wholly working class culture. But it is sufficient for this narration to concentrate on the period from which the Methodist Church decided that the Wythenshawe churches should be recognised as a 'priority appointment'; terminology applied to the process used in the appointment of a new Methodist minister.

As far as the authoritative voice of the Methodist Church was concerned, the churches for various reasons were beyond saving bar one. Not surprisingly, it was suggested that four of the churches might best be closed and their membership transferred to the one that remained open and that was the message and presumably the task conveyed to the prospective superintendent minister. Such an idea as this was ruminated without a proper professional assessment and neither with proper consultation with the people from the five churches involved. So, according to the due process for priority appointments, a superintendent minister was indeed selected and appointed to serve the five

Methodist churches in Wythenshawe from September 1998 and that person specifically earmarked and commissioned, was me.

Following my appointment as the new superintendent minister (the senior minister with oversight of the circuit) and with no time to lose, a comprehensive survey was carried out from which a detailed plan of a possible new future was presented to the churches. It is worth noting that the survey included consultations with all church denominations on the housing estate, social services in their myriad operational formularies, statutory and vocational organisations involved in social regeneration, local authority housing, schools and establishments associated with health care besides local councillors and voluntary organisations.

The 'Plan' as it became known gave detailed information on how each of the churches could proceed towards new future ministries and by necessity, under-go major refurbishment. The key to this was engagement to the point of working relationships with non-church organisations whose primary mission would be social regeneration of one form or another. The sheer compilation of this new strategic approach of church mission and ministry on a large working class housing estate and written up in the form of a comprehensive plan conversant with church members, had Kingdom of God principles inscribed all over it.

The acceptance of the Plan by all five churches gave the go-ahead for such a new future for the churches not based on old systems and past activities, but on the values embedded in the theology of the Kingdom of God. It was acknowledged at this beginning of the initial stage that not all participating bodies and future stake holders would be aware or appraised of the important contribution Kingdom of God theology would be rendering to the future shape and mission of the whole enterprise. One way to highlight the principle points of Kingdom of God theology and values in their application to the five churches was to differentiate them from the more contemporary mission initiatives and theological approach by the majority of churches today. A simple comparison is even noticeable in Methodist churches or in Methodist Circuit Mission Statements, an example of which is apparent in these two mission statements, the first one by an anonymous Methodist Circuit and the second one by our own Wythenshawe Circuit:

EXAMPLE NO: 1

We are a circuit whose faith is:

- Celebrated in worship
- Committed to spiritual growth
- Expressed in sharing the good news
- Worked out with people of all ages within our communities

Together as a circuit we:

- Undertake to provide opportunities to worship God in spirit and in truth
- Undertake to encourage each other in our journey of discipleship
- Are committed to serving others and by sharing our faith encouraging others into discipleship
- Will seek to work with Christians and churches of other traditions to further the work of the gospel.

EXAMPLE NO. 2

To meet the spiritual and pastoral needs of members of all five congregations by providing:

- Time and space for one to one befriending/counselling.
- Time and space for prayer, Bible study and small group work.
- Time and space for House Communions, hospital and special pastoral visits.
- Time and space for social interaction and deepening of friendship.
- Time and space for those wanting to think and reflect upon the world in a Christian context.

to provide resources for the training and encouragement of:

- Worship leaders, preachers and assistants.
- Workers with children.
- Workers involved in 'people-orientated' organisations.
- Leaders of small groups.
- By utilising knowledge, experience and know-how from the general pool of personnel in the circuit.

to be a people providing a safe refuge for:

- Vulnerable children and adults.
- The hurt and rejected in society.
- The sad, lonely and people bereaved.
- The frail and elderly.
- By offering the services of minister, lay worker and pastoral assistants.

to have a circuit identity and to be real church communities

- Where upkeep is given to church buildings.
- With interest shown and active involvement given to local neighbourhood initiatives.
- Where there is a genuine spirit of participation in the Body of Christ.

to continue and develop further the circuit's long-term plans:

- Of five distinct and 'specialised' ministries as befits future generations with...
- Re-designed premises to accommodate and promote such ministries
- Through the auspices of the Circuit Steering Group and the Circuit/Stewards Meeting
- And every available resource.

The second example being our new Wythenshawe mission statement was adopted at the beginning stages of its new initiative and before Wythenshawe Oasis was formed and before arrangements with partner organisations were made. Wythenshawe Oasis (W.O.) with charitable status was formed in 2002 in order to give principal leadership to project work, management and fund raising. Detailed information on Wythenshawe Oasis is given towards the end of this chapter.

What becomes interesting when the two mission statements are compared is the dissimilarity between the first statement and its theoretical and spiritual style, from the second statement that is more practical and human in content and intent. Appreciating these two comparisons, and especially for the purposes of establishing the role and function of the Kingdom of God in church and community life today; it is befitting to examine a little more closely what appears to be the primary aims and objectives of some churches in these times.

Chief characteristics of today's average church in relation to their overall purpose and work, appears to be thus:

- To preach a message of God's love with the intention of challenging people to accept God into their lives and attend church regularly.
- To increase the sizes of congregations and use them as the primary Christian community to which people should show allegiance.
- To appreciate a real difference between being Christian and not being Christian to the point of recognising a contrast between the two in favour of being Christian.
- To give instruction on matters of Faith based on biblical truths' which in turn leads to a particular 'Christian' life-style.
- To deepen personal spirituality through prayer and meditation, strengthen universal healing and give praise to God.
- To show appreciation for God's world especially through respect for creation, in care and concern for people in need and through support to charities doing good works.

In contrast, the chief characteristics that underpinned the plan for the five Wythenshawe churches in their adoption of the principles and values of the Kingdom of God were thus:

- Use all available resources to fulfil a ministry to people and neighbourhood communities in need of social and spiritual regeneration.
- Use the teachings and example of Jesus in the gospels as the model and inspiration for the work of God and in a just cause for the people.
- Engage with professional and voluntary organisations plus respective personnel with whom church people can deliver much needed quality services without financial constraint to anyone.
- Alter, transform and refurbish church buildings to make them fit for use by professional and voluntary organisations with long-term leases, especially activities requiring professional equipment and purpose-built premises.
- To appreciate all people, church and non-church people alike, and any other configuration without distinction, as part of the universal family of God from which Christ-like sister and brother relationships can flourish.
- To encourage congregations to use Sunday worship for the purposes of Kingdom of God teaching, to give a real sense of belonging, and to be a spiritual foundation to everything that happens as part of Christ's mission.

- To take seriously the call of Christ to live the sacrificial life, to be a servant to all, to stand up for justice, support the weak, show 'agape' love especially to the vulnerable and in all things be sincere.

The chief characteristics of the Kingdom of God employed in the development work and in the every-day ministries ensued, is best described as incorporating into church project work the intrinsic nature of Christ's teaching on the Kingdom of God, to the extent that it determined the character of the project work. Examples and clarification of this is an on-going discourse of this writing, but simple illustrations would pin-point Christ's universal appeal, that the Kingdom he was inaugurating was for all people without discrimination or the need for qualification; the Kingdom of God was to be international and multi-cultural in its inclusion of all people. By the same token, the work of the churches especially through the project work was likewise open to all people and by necessity that meant offering specialist services and facilities of the highest quality. To people with autism, people with a speech impediment or with low self-esteem, people with mental health issues, ex-offenders, people in need of counselling, and the list goes on. These people and many others requiring special pastoral and professional care were served and their needs met, not merely by accident or by good fortune alone, but because the 'services' were set up and became designed to give social and spiritual benefit as demonstrated and taught by Christ through his own 'service-led' work.

Such was the Kingdom of God approach which proved to have an unequivocal and universal appeal. Not surprisingly, it was entirely appropriate as a template for the Wythenshawe churches situated as they were on one of the largest housing estates in Europe and living, breathing a working class culture. Its use as a template is best illustrated by pin-pointing salient facts that highlight some of the chief characteristics of working class culture in cross reference to examples drawn from Christ's own ministry.

WORKING CLASS CULTURE AND CHRIST'S OWN MINISTRY

The variety of identifying points of personal contact numerously illustrated in the gospels and drawn largely from Christ's conversations and encounters, his healing ministry and miracles, insights gained from his personal example and knowledge gleaned from consequential circumstances that impacted upon him, are inexhaustible. They create a myriad of facts and information about people from a cross section of backgrounds, circumstances and life-styles; and it is when these characteristics, including their self-image, idiosyncrasies, desires and ambitions, are observed that an appreciation of their worth can be comprehended and a sense of community cohesion acknowledged and understood. The same perspective can be applied to Wythenshawe people with very similar results. They are a cross section of people drawn from a common background with huge potential to make personal relationships of substance, with a desire to be part of a community identity. In time this became a catalyst for individuals to be recognised for the people they were, for the individual gifts they possessed and for the contribution they were able to give to the common good.

Those who have not had the benefits of a good all-round education which is a common characteristic on housing estates, discover much about the Christian faith when they are involved in practical tasks and pursuits and place their endeavours alongside not dissimilar examples found in the gospel narratives. This also gives a much needed boost to self-esteem as well as giving day-by-day encouragement, an all-important sense of purpose with a vision and an enterprise that is always worth achieving. It is important to note that these same characteristics are closely identified with similar characteristics involving individuals highlighted in Christ's own ministry.

This way of aligning oneself to the Christian faith, through hands-on practical task orientated work or project-based activities and endeavours, introduces a wide range of practitioners lay and ordained, to a form of pilgrimage where they find themselves in a common heritage among fellow pilgrims. Instead of a classical pilgrimage featuring a physical journey where the journey's end becomes the destiny, the Wythenshawe pilgrimage had its own spiritual journey shared also with fellow pilgrims and not with just one overall destination, but a journey with many destinies. It is often the case that it is in the doing of the practical Christian work that individuals discover or at least reveal, an inner spiritual characteristic and in time, especially in the setting of consistent 'journeying'. It is not untypical for that individual to show signs of Christlikeness. The 'destinies' can be times of personal and particular achievements, the opening up of personal qualities that have been hidden or unnoticed, changes in personality or new-found values, long sought-after changes in personal circumstances and difficult situations. All these 'destinies' not withstanding the concept of the pilgrimage itself, play a very significant part in an individual's or a community of people's (pilgrims) acknowledgement of the long established Christian message and most importantly, the embodiment of the principles and values encompassed and expressed in the Kingdom of God itself. A realisation of what it means to a 'fellow pilgrim', as I have described them, is spelt out in the chapter that includes 'Portraits of Unforgettable People'.

Accepting the overwhelming need for the Wythenshawe churches to be service-led with as much professionalism as possible, the 'pilgrimage' principles, applied also to the organisations and personnel with whom serious partnerships were formed. Spiritual nuances became apparent in various members of staff, as well as in different teams of workers; and this was right across the board from professional pay-roll personnel, to volunteers, cleaners, caretakers and administrators. By virtue of necessity, a list of craftsmen and contractors required for all kinds of utility work was held and they were always being called upon to oversee property maintenance. And most of these contracted workers were also part of that shared Wythenshawe pilgrimage, particularly those who practiced a philosophical premise that was in sympathy with Kingdom of God values. But what was most discernible was the Christian and spiritual ethos that underpinned the vast majority of project work, involving the activities, task orientated pursuits and services commissioned and delivered by church and partner organisations alike.

The key to positive interaction between all the people associated with the proliferation of the multiple enterprises can be summed up in one word: 'relationship'. This included everyone: church people, personnel from partner organisations, recipients of therapeutic enhanced activities, members of the vast number of participating organisations, not to mention the plethora of Wythenshawe people who were always coming and going (being recipients or volunteers). At the heart of good relationships is trust, honesty, sincerity, comradeship, understanding, an interest in one another's stories, a desire to give of oneself and in return to have the good grace to likewise receive from others. Examples of relationships such as these are numerous and many of them are catalogued in the different narratives of this thesis. They range from chief executives of organisations and Trusts, business managers, co-ordinators, independent practitioners, leaders of voluntary organisations, dedicated volunteers, to individuals and groups of people outside Wythenshawe and only indirectly involved, but whose consistent reassurance was like a never ending stream of encouragement and source of strength.

It is positively fascinating as well as being a source of inspiration, to discover the many and varied relationships Christ entered into and were considered essential. They reveal his gift and ability to enter into dialogue with the whole spectrum of society, from the most noble to the true lowliest, from the most notorious sinner to the genuine enquirer, from the ulterior motive enemy to the compassionate acquaintance, from the person with disabilities or mental health issues to fellow disciples and vast congregations. In other words, Christ's relationships whether in the form of one-to-ones, or as in a family setting, or as a collective of people, his hall-mark and approved standard was integral with his own integrity. As well as being something positive and 'healing' or 'therapeutic' or 'good advice' or 'mutually beneficial', Christ's encounters were all part and parcel of the working out and expansion of the Kingdom of God.

Likewise, relationships with all those engaged in the work of God affiliated to and identified with the five Wythenshawe Methodist churches, found their raison d'etre in the fundamental values of the Kingdom of God. Whether talked through or not, whether the overriding principles were constituted or not, whether the work and relationships were bathed in formal prayers or not, whether there were differences of opinion or not, whether everyone went to church and professed to be Christian or not, integrity was key and a real sense of pilgrimage and mission over and beyond human endeavour was the end result.

The reason why there was still a Methodist presence in Wythenshawe in 1998 was mainly due to the church buildings, in that they had not already closed down. That each of the five church properties was in a very poor state of repair and their congregation's small and on the whole made up of elderly people, was a fact. Small and elderly they may have been, but it must not be overlooked that the church people were more than capable of emanating the presence of Christ and vital that was too. Unsurprisingly therefore, it was that situation which created what became a preoccupying consideration and on reflection, was neatly framed-up in one word: 'potential'. Irrespective of their need for structural repair and serious refurbishment, the church buildings and not least the congregations small as they were, presented an opportunity and a challenge not to be missed. To make possible the work of the Kingdom of God as envisaged, required premises and in many instances, purpose-built facilities too. There could not have been a better reason to draw up plans that would in time, involve a major refurbishment in all five church properties. At the same time, the five small congregations would fulfil a most important role by being supportive towards potential partner organisations, by showing an interest in the services they would be offering and by sharing a mutual spiritual approach in all things. This gave unlimited scope and one which was capitalised upon over the succeeding years as the plans with partner organisations took shape, the service-led enterprises began to be developed and the church buildings went through their transformations.

CHAPTER 2:
THE KINGDOM OF GOD; ITS PRINCIPLES AND VALUES

This chapter describes the way we organised a new administrative base and its identity with the Believers cited in the Acts of the Apostles, the formation of partnerships with organisations and the place of the values associated with the Kingdom of God.

From drawing board to actuality

GETTING ORGANISED AND THE ACTS OF THE APOSTLES

It was obvious from the beginning that none of the five Methodist churches could stand alone and fulfil all the administrative responsibilities including, the maintenance of their buildings / premises and neither could they manage the legal niceties in the constitutional arrangements with partner organisations as single churches; a fact that became more compelling as the projects and ministries grew and developed. It was for these reasons and to maximise the opportunity to share resources that it was agreed a collective approach between all churches would produce the best results. The pilot scheme for this approach was the formation of the original circuit steering group that consisted of two representatives from each church plus co-opted personnel. That beginning of collective responsibility steered the way for future methods of working, including eventually one church council for all five churches. The case for this innovative scheme of operation can best be summarised for the following reasons:

- Lack of skill and expertise among the small congregations to fulfil administrative tasks in today's high tech and modern management systems of bureaucracy.

- The duties and responsibilities of office holders and the authority invested in them was asking too much of people inexperienced handling such personal accountability.

- Small congregations on their own felt too vulnerable and weak considering the day-to-day oversight required from them. But when representatives of all five churches came together and they exercised appropriate oversight collectively, they felt strong and confident and were able to give the leadership required of them.

- On the occasions when individual churches needed help, support and encouragement, the structure of the five church organisations was already in place to meet the needs and to share the much valued human and practical resources.

- Having a centralised and well equipped operational office with skilled staff enabled the churches to retain their own autonomy, whilst at the same time appreciate the value of staff that could handle the administrative burdens and fulfil a consultative role with the churches.

- A centralised office fulfilled an important 'professional' role especially in relation to statutory partner organisations because they required a recognisable level of professionalism.

- Having a central base was an asset for all-round good communication and for the publication of newsletters, periodicals, events and the exchange of church and project news and updates.

- This collective approach, assisted by office personnel, large and small items of equipment, furniture, general resources, and essential hands-on volunteers, was not only an essential form of sharing but something easy to co-ordinate.

Such sharing of skills and resources was common-place and played an essential role in equipping projects in their work and in forwarding a shared pilgrimage. The image in Acts 4:32 of the believers sharing their possessions and pooling their personal wealth and likewise in chapter 2:42 in the way they were mutually supportive in the development of their spirituality and charitable actions, was used to a degree as a model for the five churches. Emphasis on the building up of one another in faith, fellowship and parity was an important component and to achieve overall success required a structure that would enable good administration, good management and unimpeded participation to flourish. The following structure for a workable organisation was created:

1. **A combined Church Stewards' meeting.**

   This was for church officials (stewards) from the five churches and was primarily the setting for mutual sharing of business, ideas and encouragement.

2. **A Circuit Leadership Meeting.**

   This was held three times a year and consisted of a small group of people drawn from the churches to share ideas for circuit (combined) events, get them organised and carry out tasks as and when required.

3. **Church Meetings at each of the 5 churches.**

   These were held every three months and took the place of a Sunday Service. They were open to everyone who happened to be in the congregation and as such, everyone was included. Everyone had a voice and all voices were heard. The meeting's primary aim was to oversee the day-to-day life of the church, its activities, project work, worship and spiritual matters, pastoral care, engagement with their local neighbourhood and programme of future work. An annual meeting was held which would receive a variety of reports and make appointments.

4. **A Combined Church Council.**

   These were held every four months and their primary purpose was to oversee the following: Legal matters including leases, governance including appointments, finances, church property, including alterations, refurbishment and maintenance, insurance including claims, annual schedules and audits, safeguarding measures and the welfare of the churches generally. For procedural purposes, each church was named and a set of questions was asked of the church in relation to the governance the meeting was obliged to adhere to. The fascinating detail that nearly always emerged from that process was the sheer help and encouragement that was given to each church by the meeting as a whole. Instead of individual churches coping completely on their own as they did as single church councils, the hopes, aspirations and frustrations often experienced by the churches became the responsibility of everyone and that was never exercised lightly. This denotes a clear connection with the 'believers' cited in Acts chapters 2 and 4.

5. **The Circuit Meeting.**

This meeting was held three times a year with the primary aim of helping all five churches to live out their own aims and objectives. It took with absolute seriousness the felicity and prospects of the churches and considered all programmes of ministry and mission, organised combined events involving all five churches and was responsible for all paid staff including ministers. The Circuit Meeting was the official body commissioned to exercise authority and responsibility concerning everything associated with the five Wythenshawe Churches.

6. **Wythenshawe Oasis**

As a charity, Wythenshawe Oasis (WO) is an independent trust in its own right and can therefore act as such. In reality it identifies, co-operates and works with all five churches. WO has its own onstitution with aims and objectives that it fulfils through its programmes of project work with the churches and the churches' partner organisations. WO founding principle was to redress poverty through community programmes of re-generation and to be a practical resource to the Wythenshawe churches. As such the charity established a WO committee consisting of personnel from Wythenshawe churches and from the world of commerce and social enterprise. WO primary functions are:

- Work with personnel from the churches and partner organisations in the development and delivery of specific projects.
- Raise money to fund the projects.
- Help organise management systems to run the projects.
- Help in the monitoring process of the projects.
- Oversee WO website.

- Assist in WO publicity and give guidance to church project publicity.

In all, thousands and thousands of £s were raised and funds came from a variety of grant making bodies, all of which came under the heading of social regeneration of one kind or another. These included government grants operated through local authorities, a whole mixture of trusts gleaned from the directory of grant making trusts, some through the auspices of partner organisations' sources of funding and others from church, organisations and personal donations. Of particular value were funds initiated by influential trustees known and inspired through our endeavours and some of these were exceptionally large grants repeated over a period of three or more years. The real worth of all these funds was clearly seen in the generosity of individual people who believed in the work we were doing and gave their unstinting support.

Throughout the vast majority of WO life, it has enjoyed good and progressive working relationships with churches and partner organisations, achieved not by accident but by design. It has always been imperative that WO personnel enjoyed excellent relationships with all those with whom it worked and carried out its primary objectives.

Among the large and diverse team of managers, administrators, technicians and volunteers two roles in particular stand out namely: the Administrator and the Chair of Wythenshawe Oasis. They stand out because of the brief they exercised and the authority invested in them. On the one hand it seems quite incongruous to single two roles from all the others when there was a parity of importance spread across the whole team, but on the other hand, the work of the overall administrator and that of the chair of Wythenshawe Oasis were exceptional and require particular explanation.

7. **The Administrator.**

The administrator for the churches was also WO administrator and this combined role was essential for quality co-ordination and efficiency. The office base for both enterprises was St. Andrew's House which proved highly successful in networking and liaison operations and in the co-ordination of on-going project work and enterprises. This was a much valued arrangement as the administrator would always be cross referencing with WO managers and volunteers, local church officers and national church officials and not least with partner organisations and would team them up with one another as and when appropriate, as well as fulfilling the expected requirement of administrative services.

A significant amount of church administration especially in relation to property repairs, break-ins, hiring of premises, preparation of leases and administering letting forms, utilities, finance, annual reports and surveys was mostly handled by the Administrator in liaison with local church stewards or officers. Not only did this keep everything running smoothly and efficiently, but it relieved the churches of a burden at times too overwhelming for them and also created a bridge between the churches over which much inter-communication and net-working took place.

Another useful and important role was that of receptionist/facilitator. As a community house as well as being the office base for the churches and Wythenshawe Oasis, the administrator was 'on tap' for callers and visitors and could be the friendly face especially at times when people needed a lot of tender loving care. A facilitating role was most useful and it often doubled up to provide pastoral care as well; notably in sorting out the complex form filling and rental regulations with asylum seekers, besides a particular case which required working through the administrative system in order to get someone installed in social housing. On numerous occasions and in a variety of ways the Administrator provided valuable service as Pastor, host and mentor.

8. **Wythenshawe Oasis Chairperson**
Throughout WO major enterprising period, the Chairperson was also the superintendent minister for the five churches. This dual role was used to maximum advantage and effect among all the staff, all the

enterprises, commercial contractors, interested parties and personnel from the influential world of public relations.

The contribution of WO to the on-going re-generative work cannot be over-estimated, nor its work and involvement with churches and partner organisations. Together with the churches and partner organisations, WO was the third part of the triangle that made possible the implementation of the principles and values of the Kingdom of God. It made sure the practical resources were in place and operational so the various projects could become a means of blessing for the people. This industrious period of work in its triangular operational format, illustrated the values and principles that provided the cohesion within the trinity. The similarities in philosophical approach were most noticeable in meeting the needs of the people, irrespective of circumstance; in being one in heart and mind; in the mutual comradeship that was nurtured; in the inclusive communities it fostered; in the churches not claiming their possessions as their own but sharing everything they had, even to the point of making physical alterations to the buildings to accommodate specialised services; and in the subtle ways 'grace' as the free and unmerited favour of God shown towards humankind, became a very human reality. The personification of that grace was revealed in the way the vast majority of 'workers' (staff & volunteers) applied and approached their work. It was in their attitude, in their manner, in their chosen methods, in their whole modus operandi, all of which should not be surprising if the true principles and values of the Kingdom of God were indeed underpinning everything.

It was crucial to the success of the overall vision to make sure every opportunity to expand and develop was exploited and made possible to the fullest degree. As the superintendent minister of the churches and the Chair of W.O. this was always achieved with admirable co-ordination between all the various stake-holders and excellent co-operation between the many church and partner organisations.

It could be considered unusual to associate non-church organisations and people in the working out of the Kingdom of God but, the similarities with the Believers methodology in Acts does not make it unusual at all in the context of the work at Wythenshawe. The meaning and implications in the declaration in Acts 4:32: 'all the believers were one in heart and mind', was key to the formation of working relationships among all the different Wythenshawe organisations and individuals. There was nothing casual or accidental about the relationships; they were born out of a common purpose, written up in constitutions and mission statements and lived out in serious ways to improve people's health, welfare and overall life-styles. The cohesion that cemented the relationships was the same spiritual grace that gave worth and meaning to the 'being one in heart and mind'. And often organisations as well as the churches needed the strength, guidance and support of the others during times of particular weakness or difficulty and not least a corporate joy in the celebration of success.

Talking about the theories of working relationships of a practical hands-on nature is far from an easy exercise. Conversations and consultations either in a more formal setting of a meeting, or as and when needs arose between partner organisations, occurred all the time; and it is interesting that by far the commonest reason for them is best described as pastoral concerns. For example, someone from Studio One, with a mental health issue which, by its very nature is handled within the realm of confidentiality, is given a volunteer's role in Mo's shop, and, crucially, placed where important pastoral supervisory attention is also on hand. The placement addressed both the social and its mental health needs of the volunteers. (Mo's shop is elucidated in chapter 5) This level of conversation and decision-making among the leadership of groups and organisations, giving due respect to the need for confidentiality, was a common feature. Aspects of shared pastoral care of that depth and quality, alongside the every-day business and organisational responsibilities were always being exchanged. As the minister and go-between person, I knew about that level of inter-personal communication only too well. The important element of human worth and spiritual integrity, both of which were exercised and recognised, comes very close indeed to the comradeship of the believers quoted from Acts of the Apostles "All the believers were one in heart and mind." All the organisations were indeed of one heart and mind.

It was this hallmark which gave the relationships a spiritual depth and a future around which all participating bodies and agencies could play their respective part, in the work of the Kingdom of God.

THE ROLE OF PARTNER ORGANISATIONS

The task for the five local churches was straightforward: Think of one specific area of work that will become a specialist area of mission, ministry or community activity and find organisations with appropriate skills, resources etc. that will develop that project with you.

Inspiration for this came from Luke's account of the Roman Centurion (Luke 7:1-10). Through the Centurion's involvement in the building of the synagogue and compassion he showed towards his sick and dying servant, the Centurion revealed all the signs of being a participator or a co-worker in what Jesus described as the Kingdom of God.

Forming partnerships with organisations to deliver specific services especially when they were of a specialist nature and intended for people usually unable to access them, enabled the churches to pursue and fulfil ministries that would have been impossible to do on their own. As these specialist areas of work increased so too did the concept that the Kingdom of God knew no bounds and the partner organisations facilitating them through the churches began to show clear signs of a growing spirituality.

As this work with partner organisations grew and the value of their involvement intensified, the church communities themselves discovered a new purpose for being a church. And their relationships with the organisations became a sharing of responsibilities the churches previously, had to manage and administer on their own.

The specialist nature of the work by many of the partner organisations required the churches to make substantial and radical alterations to their premises and in order to embark upon such schemes of co-operation, long-term lease agreements were required. This gave the church's ministries a veracity and virtue which multiplied in countless blessings, and made possible the make-overs of the buildings that were long over-due.

Other signs of the Kingdom of God were particularly noticeable in the actual day-to-day work of the respective ministries and through the inter-personal relationships with all participators including professional members of staff, volunteer helpers and the participants (clients) themselves. Kingdom of God values and insights into their distinctive characters became more and more discernible in the partner organisations especially through the enthusiasm and vocation-like will of all involved, and in the joy and exhilaration displayed.

In many instances this new focus for the churches became also a new focus for the partner organisations, the only difference being in terminology. In describing particular outcomes of their work, organisations used terms such as: 'empowerment', 'social inclusion', 'programmes of involvement', 'community regeneration', 'increasing self-esteem' etc. At the same time the churches increasingly referred to this new approach of church work and the newness of the enterprises being delivered, as the inclusive work of the Kingdom of God. The contemporary and familiar terms used by churches to express their church work, eg: 'mission', 'ministry', 'outreach', 'discipleship' etc. were surpassed by the one title: 'Kingdom of God'.

KINGDOM VALUES

When serious consideration is given to the expectations rooted in Kingdom of God values, something becomes inescapable. It is the need to go one extra mile after another. This should not be an unfamiliar expectation and neither something arduous to a tried and tested Methodist, because they will be accustomed to the call to 'give all of themselves' in the name of God and for the purposes of serving Christ. The Annual Covenant Service is the one identifiable hallmark of what is required to be a Methodist and establishes unequivocally time honoured expectations, expectations that are signed and sealed in a re-affirmation of a Covenant relationship between themselves and God. This extract from the Covenant Service reveals the depth of meaning in the self-sacrificial nature of that commitment and the willingness always to go one extra mile after another: "I am no longer my own but yours. Your will, not mine, be done in all things, wherever you may place me, in all that I do and in all that I may endure... Your will be done when I am valued and when I am disregarded; when I find fulfilment and when it is lacking; when I have all things, and when I have nothing. I willingly offer all I have and am to serve you, as and where you choose." It cannot be surprising therefore to read in the Wythenshawe Churches statement of intent, the call to a servant-style sacrificial life whereby justice in all things is upheld, the weak and the vulnerable are always supported and sincerity is a must. These are Kingdom of God values and it was crucial that they permeated through the very beings of everyone associated with the work of the Kingdom of God and with those for whatever reasons had made a connection with us.

Close examination of these Kingdom values reveals high expectations of people and a lot of dogged hard work too. Understandably, the end result was mixed. The majority of volunteers including church people and non-church people alike, clearly did roll their sleeves up, right up to their elbows, got stuck in and worked solidly and in a way that made their dedication to the cause unmistakeable. A similar commitment by a goodly number of staff from partner organisations especially those in managerial positions likewise, demonstrated a commitment that had spiritual depth written all over it. Another segment of people deeply interested in our enterprises and initiatives and showed in a form of dedication to us as a people, were those from nearby churches, individuals from far and wide and souls who, on the whole, were restricted to their homes. They found their own unique ways to be consistent in the giving of their help and support and by so doing, in unison with all the others, exhibited their own allegiances.

The Methodist Covenant Service, let alone the bidding embodied in the Kingdom of God itself, is first and foremost an appeal for individual sincerity and everything else that follows is from a standpoint of self-denial, put in theological terms; following the way of the cross. If as it seemed, a large part of the negativity by the Methodist Church towards Wythenshawe, was paranoia about taking risks, the only risk was in the decision, either to follow the way of the Covenant Service and the Kingdom of God or not. There being no other choice, Wythenshawe churches, partner organisations and the host of volunteers chose to honour the Methodist Church by being true to its Covenant and through sheer loyalty to Christ, embraced everything that had anything to do with God's Kingdom.

It is when serious consideration is given to the role and purpose of the church in terms of its mission and outreach on a large housing estate, that major deliberation needs to be given to everything associated with the people's prevailing culture and cultural life-style. Such an exercise needs to include the people's background, their work, disposition, opportunities or lack of them and the overall framework that houses their belief systems and establishes the kind of society they are. In other words an examination of a demographic survey of the estate would be essential, in order to understand and show proper respect to the people and at the same time discover the best ways to form relationships with them. It is essential because cultural configurations vary enormously and the chosen methods of interaction within a predominantly working class ethic have their own distinct attributes.

It was with those attributes in mind that the statement of intent, the churches' mission statement and the overall plans for the entire advancement of work were drawn up and subsequently followed through. That is why there appears a stark contrast between the Wythenshawe statement of intent and the statement of intent that is descriptive of many churches today. Having considered the statement drawn up for the Wythenshawe situation, it is important and illuminating to observe the style and content of statements that are presented by what seems to be a large number of churches today.

Whilst the approach employed by the five Wythenshawe churches towards Wythenshawe people has been proven to be wholly appropriate and successful in being a living entity of the Kingdom of God, it does not mean there cannot be other approaches different from Wythenshawe's that may likewise be appropriate for their particular situations and contexts. But it is the claim of this thesis that the Kingdom of God approach for housing estates and working class communities like that of Wythenshawe, carries an integrity of purpose and intent in its mission and ministry by its people to its people, that singularly justifies its methodology, its practice and its faithfulness to its calling to be and do the work of Christ.

Whilst appreciating and accepting the need to get alongside the culture and cultural life-style of Wythenshawe people, it is important to gain the maximum interaction and understanding as possible; and much encouragement should be given to anyone involved in work similar to what we were doing. The following bullet pointed paragraphs are useful considerations for achieving such a rapport and identity:

- Give due recognition of a cultural lifestyle unique to a working class society with a willingness and desire to interact within that habitat.

- Discovering common ground and capitalising upon its significance.

- Being relaxed, comfortable and at ease in a working class environment and setting.

- Using the powers of empathy whenever possible and appropriate.

- Being easy going and friendly in peoples' company.

- Giving consideration to people too frequently feeling they are side-lined by officialdom and achieving it by showing a genuine interest at the same time as giving the people priority over time and other less important considerations.

- Gaining knowledge on how and why people have low self-esteem and those who physically harm themselves so they can be befriended appropriately and help be given to them to gain self-respect.

- Recognising the signs in people with learning difficulties and helping them acquire the same opportunities as other people.

- Making sure opportunities to mix and mingle with people are taken up.

- Remembering personal details about people; even the more minor aspects of conversations and acknowledging them on subsequent occasions.

- Creating situations whereby people are not only welcomed but they know they are welcome.

- Making sure meeting-points or the environment for conviviality is conducive and favourable to the person or people concerned.

- Work from the principle and belief that there is always the potential for something good and worthy in everyone, despite circumstances that may suggest otherwise.

- Discover appropriate settings to meet people appreciating when unorthodox or unconventional locations may be an advantage.

- Be properly prepared and briefed before meetings and show unbiased sensitivity to all views.

- Be professional in the conduct of business among professionals with whom working relationships are important.

- Show respect towards partner organisations and acknowledge them as equals and colleagues.

- Be aware of conveying a patronising manner and the subtle way it can be adversely conveyed.

- Discern spiritual characteristics in people, in community activities and organisations especially in non-church traditional environments.

- Acknowledgement that the Kingdom of God is diverse and can operate in unseen ways and situations as well as in ways which are identifiable.
- The ability and desire to relate today's human stories and happenings with stories in the gospels and vice versa.

It is the case that many of these distinguishing features practised by volunteer and professional practitioners from church and community socially orientated work, are found in a variety of cultural settings. It remains however that they are vital characteristics when engaged in work and relationships among a people earthed in a working class culture and out of sheer necessity, it is essential they are accompanied with genuine sensitivity and courtesies.

The requirement of such 'genuine sensitivity and courtesies' towards people of a working class culture become apparent, when serious consideration is given to their particular personal characteristics, derived as they are from the uniqueness of their inherent culture. Key factors that distinguish their character and give shape to individual personalities can be appreciated by considering an individual's negative characteristics in comparison with their positive attributes:

Negative characteristics:

- Low educational attainment.
- Low self-esteem.
- Lack of confidence.
- Unemployment.
- Little or no peer support.
- Speech impediment
- Living and coping with learning difficulties.
- Absence of role models.
- Victim of abuse.
- Grown up in an abusive family household.
- History of being bullied.
- Sufferer of nervous anxiety.
- Homelessness.
- Severe relationship problems with stepfathers, parents, foster carers.
- Under influence of drugs.
- Having served time in H.M.P.
- Self-harming.
- Loss of trust in people.

- Living in fear of partner &/or family members.
- Being in debt and inability to manage personal finance.
- Living with an addiction.
- Lack of experience outside immediate environment.
- Dyslexia and limited reading and writing skills.
- Feelings of tension and anxiety in environment outside natural habitat.
- Loss of self-esteem due to being placed in unfamiliar / formal setting.
- Difficulty understanding red tape from authoritative bodies.
- Being vulnerable and exploitative.
- Inability to stand up for self.
- Easy to be down-trodden.
- Phobias.
- Health problems
- Weight problems
- Low appreciation of self-worth and abilities.

Any one or more of these examples can too easily contribute to a negative attitude that becomes part of the individual concerned.

Positive attributes:

- Having no airs and graces.
- Feeling 'at home' in ordinary settings.
- Being naturally humble.
- Contentment with unsophisticated life-style.
- Hard working.
- Sincerity.
- Keen to be a voluntary helper
- Honesty and openness in conversation.
- Warm-hearted.
- Welcoming.
- Generous in spirit and friendship
- Self-assured in natural environment.
- Prepared to take initiative under good leadership
- Acceptance of responsibilities with assistance.
- Good sense of humour.
- Demonstrative of appreciation.
- Always at the ready to do practical tasks.

- Genuine desire to be involved and included.
- Having the qualities described as being 'the salt of the earth'.
- Potentiality.
- Gifted and talented.
- Leadership qualities.
- Consistent and dependable.
- Givers as well as receivers.
- Trusting nature.
- Enjoys conviviality of peer group.
- Love a good party.
- Resourceful participators in community events.
- Strong willed.
- Simple uncluttered approach to life.
- Spiritual presence discernible in their personalities.
- Possession of personal qualities that go unnoticed.
- An identity with characters highlighted in Christ's parables and encounters.
- A natural spiritual quality.
- A capacity to empathise.

Likewise, it is these positive attributes that can release potential and embolden the individual in creative and expressive ways.

An in-depth exploration of many of the characters portrayed in the synoptic gospels including actual people encountered by Christ himself, or symbolically portrayed in parabolic stories, reveal a closeness to many of today's working class people. Add to them the personality types emphasised in Christ's teaching especially from the Sermon on the Mount in Matthew and the negative and positive features attributed to working class people, give credibility to a personal identity or affinity with the biblical personality types singled out. Such gospel characters whether brought to life through story, personal encounter or teaching, are encompassed in that new setting or habitat Christ called the Kingdom of God. Whether a certain affinity with the gospel characters as discussed is experienced or not, or known or not, many of todays' Wythenshawe people inhabit or dwell in that same Kingdom of God. And whether through church ministry or through spiritual regeneration or through social cohesion of one kind or another, when this theological and spiritual approach is positively promoted by the church, the Kingdom of God is not something that just happens to be there. It is a living cell upon which everything else is woven together as in the making of a tapestry, except the tapestry in this instance is clearly: the Kingdom of God tapestry.

Before giving detailed consideration of the service-led 'ministries' that became part and parcel of the work of the Kingdom of God, it is salient to recall the part played by the churches' previous ministries concerning the people and the housing estate as a whole. For ease of definition they are listed under the following headings:

1. **Social Formation**

   The churches' worship services and weekday activities played a crucial role in helping the new tenants and residents 'find their feet' on this new housing estate which was expanding all the time. Through their activities, the churches helped people get to know one another, feel less isolated amidst their new surroundings; and in the case of the Catholic Church, schools were established and social clubs formed. All the new churches quickly developed a plethora of organisations, clubs and activities. In these ways, the churches from the beginning were instrumental in creating social cohesion and laying the foundations of an 'estate ethos' consisting of comradeship and a disposition that positively encouraged responsible 'ownership' of the estate in its every-day life.

2. **Leadership**

   Every organisation, every club and every activity required leaders and leaders that would 'shepherd' the individuals and families who joined in or became signed-up members. Within that 'leadership' there was personal and pastoral care given and received, as well as good governance employed in the running of the associations. Such leaders often became recognised responsible 'advocates' for their fellow citizen's welfare and the general needs of the estate, as well as being role-models especially for the younger generation with the addition of important 'counselling' and befriending skills.

3. **Spiritual Enrichment**

   The churches through their teaching taught and encouraged a Christian life-style and spiritual approach to situations and relationships. In this way the values and other expressions of the Kingdom of God featured prominently in the people's overall behaviour and prevailing attitudes. Churches also took the lead in co-ordinating inter-organisation activities which helped people mix among a wider network of people and through sporty organisations especially in competitive activities. The Whit Walks were a good example of this co-operative spirit and were nothing less than community togetherness that was full of enterprise, recreation and creativity; as the annual events galvanised people in their thousands in something similar in their day to the Notting Hill Carnivals of today.

4. Relationships

Through all the different meeting-points for people and families under the auspices of the churches: relationships that enhanced friendships of trust and support were formed and many of them lasted a life-time. Without relationships such as these, insecurity and vulnerability among individuals and families could easily have become prevalent. Good relationships meant there was a sharing of ideas as well as concerns, sharing of advice before it was too late and sharing of neighbourly interest; a prime example being mutual help in domestic and garden servicing.

5. Welfare and Felicity

Church organisations and especially Sunday Schools provided a raft of beneficiaries and not least among them was a genuine sense of care towards individuals. To take just one example; the leader of a church Women's Bright Hour as it was called, had around a hundred members on her books and every birthday was remembered and celebrated besides visiting members pastorally when they were poorly. This was over and above the weekly programme of meetings, invitations to speakers, the refreshments and other administrative arrangements. A similar example of immense impact made upon individuals, peer groups and families is manifest from the testimony of the churches' youth work and Sunday Schools. The membership of Methodist Youth Clubs alone, were in their hundreds and the exciting programme of activities and events year on year were second to none. This was the pattern and commitment by the leadership of numerous church organisations and shows a duty of care and schooling to a vast network of people and neighbourhoods besides the children, young people and adults named on church membership lists. In these activities and through this intense work of yesteryear when the churches were at the forefront of community development, the Kingdom of God as identified and interpreted in this writing was very much in evidence and at the heart of this cutting edge ministry.

6. **The Decline**

As the years went by and one Wythenshawe generation followed another, so too the estate grew and developed its own social network of organisations and services into an ethos that became less identified with the churches and more independently characterised. It seemed the churches had fulfilled their job, achieved their mission and, as people, were less inclined to need the 'services' of the churches. The churches retreated into something of an enclave. The vast church organisations became merely a semblance of their past, the Whit Walks ceased and the churches relied more and more on the attendance of their Sunday church services in order to retain a sense of purpose. What was once an outward looking pro-active enterprise became an inward looking preservation-led operation; and this was not confined to the Methodist churches as all the churches suffered the same fate. What was needed was a new mission, a new awakening, a new way of understanding and appreciating the work of the Kingdom of God for a very different Wythenshawe, and in that spirit a new approach to church ministry with the Kingdom of God as its foundation is, as has already been stated, what the five Methodist churches endorsed.

ANECDOTES:

The television man

It had become obvious to me that the so-called television man who had made several calls purporting to repair this elderly lady's television, was a fraud. Despite paying him good money on each repair call, the fault on the television remained and his duplicity was all too clear when visiting his company's fictitious address. So we laid a trap. The next time he called so did I. Not even wanting to answer my questions concerning his so-called repairs and refusing to reimburse the falsely taken payments, he tried to make his escape but couldn't. He couldn't escape from the house because I stood in front of the door and physically stopped him whilst shouting to the householder to call the police. I knew I couldn't restrain him for long, besides which we had already progressed to hard pushing and shoving and before the inevitable uppercut to my chin could be landed, out through the door at high speed he went.

Stuck on the bridge

This was a day out for friends and families of the five churches. The driver of the double-decker bus we hired for the day had decided to take the country scenic route to our venue which was all very nice and picturesque for us passengers, but not for our outsized vehicle. It just about managed the narrow country roads and the tight bends, but when it came to a quaint narrow humped-back bridge, the bus became well and truly grounded. It was a sight to behold and an experience to ponder, imagine being spread-eagled on the floor; that's how it seemed for this double-decker. Hogging the full width of the bridge and looking totally out of place and out of character to this scenic landscape, like a giant in a dwarf's garden, required the most skilful manoeuvring to get it out of its predicament. But all's well that ends well; reaching our destination meant we saw some of the countryside at its exquisite best, as well as having a good laugh with lots of fun at someone else's expense.

CHAPTER 3:
THE KINGDOM OF GOD SEEN THROUGH INNOVATIVE PROJECT WORK

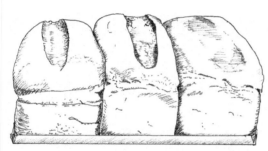

"Make bread," she said.

This chapter gives a bird's-eye view of some of the churches' projects, the way they served the people and the inter-connections between church and non-church organisations.

SERVICE-LED PROJECTS BY CHURCHES & PARTNER ORGANISATIONS

Some of the service-led organisations for whom purpose-built facilities were incorporated in the refurbishment programmes included the following:

- Alternative therapies by professional therapists with well-equipped treatment rooms in four of the churches.
- Out of School children's clubs in two of the churches.
- Community lunches, a café and a community bakery.
- A fully equipped computer suite with professional trainers and courses to match.
- Office space that accommodated administrative staff for a Healthy Living Network initiative besides a full-day's in-house programme of activities.

- Youth activities in all five churches.
- A professional counselling service.
- Art groups in two of the churches.
- Groups for adults with a programme of social activities and spiritual input held in four of the churches.
- A speech and drama class.
- A school of dancing.
- A T Dance group.
- Irish dancing groups and chair exercise classes in two of the churches.
- A well-equipped theatre with five week long highly accomplished performances per year; plus a small community-based theatrical group.
- A purpose-built and professionally run day centre for people with autism.
- An innovative and highly creative art studio for a diversity of art work including photography, textiles and needlecraft.
- A suite of premises for staff running a young people's support programme of activities including an assisted housing support scheme for young adults.
- Two lunch-time drop-in groups with assisted professional personnel.
- A well-equipped fully functional gymnasium and café bar within the setting of a therapeutic community plus a recording studio.
- An impressive and successful regular community rummage sale, known for its highly prized and quality merchandise, served as a vital resource to its local people.
- A community charity shop with its own unrivalled and down-to-earth ethos housed within its own portacabin became a lifeline to all-comers.

All of these organisations and activities besides others that are not listed played an equal or more than equal part with the churches in doing the work of the Kingdom of God. The consequence of all this enterprising work according to audited statistical figures for 2008, record a total of over 900 people being the recipients of the services offered in any one week. An account of the working practices of some of the programmes of activities by the organisations will be considered in some detail under the appropriate rubric, as will their complementary association and relationship with the work of the Kingdom of God. Suffice to say at this point, that the complementary association of service-led work with the values and principles established in Kingdom of God teaching and theology played no small part in helping to cement a real relationship with the churches' beliefs systems. It is one thing to have written up in theory an overall proposal of work, which the Wythenshawe churches did very well and did it comprehensively, but it is quite another entity to appreciate the reality of the 'togetherness relationship' enjoyed by so many, brought about by a common conviction which was and can be articulated in spiritual terms and through theological discernment.

Buildings for religious purposes during Christ's life and ministry had their uses over and above their function as places for worship and spiritual nurture. The support shown by the Roman Centurion in the building of a synagogue and recognised by the disciples, was sufficient identity with the person and purpose of Jesus, to receive in full measure Christ's affirmative acknowledgement concerning the integrity of the soldier's faith. The cleansing of the Temple by Christ, demonstrates the overwhelming need for places of religious significance to be used with discretion and with holistic reverence. In other words, they are not places that can simply be exploited for personal or commercial gain, but used for the purposes of God for the people who are the family of God.

Similarly when Jesus addressed the synagogue congregation and, with prophetic voice, simultaneously announced the inauguration of God's Kingdom alongside his own vocational intent, he brought into the heart of the synagogue and therefore the Jews' domain, those considered the least worthy, the most unclean and of no value. These included: the humble and poor, the waifs and strays, the sick and abandoned, the disadvantaged and vulnerable. It was they no less who were to be first among equals at the heart of God's Kingdom.

It was people not dissimilar to those described as being first among equals that formed the majority who accessed the many and varied services made available at the five Wythenshawe churches; and many of those services by their very nature, required suitable premises that would give permanence to the on-going work and a holistic setting that would sustain quality of service. Some personal examples of this service-led work are given elsewhere according to their appropriate settings.

The more the churches changed and adapted their premises to be fit for the purposes of their every-day work, the more the partner organisations took an interest in the general upkeep of the church buildings and their maintenance, even to the point of taking on specific responsibilities and oversight. This had obvious advantages to church communities without the necessary technical expertise, but it also gave a kind of unofficial trusteeship and sense of ownership by lease holders with theological and prophetic implications. If the work of the Kingdom of God was thus shared and thus recognised for its spiritual worth, then the premises that made it all possible, especially in the consideration that were buildings for the purposes of God, means the lease arrangements with the partner organisations in premises redesigned for their use, became a statement about a shared pilgrimage. The recognition of that shared pilgrimage was very important. It is a win-win situation all round, for the churches, for the partner organisations, for the people and for the true expansion and work of the Kingdom which Christ proclaimed. Thus, consciously or otherwise, partner organisations were participating in building God's Kingdom in Wythenshawe. This working relationship and approach is vastly different from leasing church premises merely for commercial purposes or gain. Without the initiative to develop relationships with independent organisations to the point of sharing a common purpose and pilgrimage, is a loss all round, but especially a loss to the Kingdom of God.

Church buildings were getting maximum use by organisations and visited by ever increasing numbers of people; organisations and church communities working in partnership with each other, much needed professional and voluntary services; growing communities that are not exclusive but inclusive, not uniform but diverse; all working together as one community and that community is the family of God. Being part of or a member of the family of God removes the need by churches for any other classification or membership in order to be in a relationship with God and to be in a true relationship with God's people. This is why through the work of the five Wythenshawe churches so many people from the various communities came to realise the value and benefits of being sisters and brothers to one another. It remains however that the catalyst for such an affiliation or sense of affinity boils down to an understanding of and the practicalities involved in the workings out of the Kingdom of God. To be a sister or brother to someone can be sufficient in itself, but when it is within the backdrop of the Kingdom of God, it conveys a very clear signal that the sister / brother relationship can also give a sense of rapport with the person of Christ, to the point of a personal relationship with no-one less that the person of Christ himself. Yet, the insistence by the governing authorities in the Methodist Church to categorise and name church members over and above everyone else, created serious implications and continued to remain so. It implies there are differences that become acceptable between people, that some are considered as being Christian while others are not or may not be and it more than suggests that some can be 'proper' church people and 'do things' in the name of the church, while others cannot.

Those apparently disadvantaged by practices such as these can feel, and feel acutely, a difference between themselves and those people seemingly more accepted yet equally involved in the same communities. They can feel undervalued, second-class citizens, that they are not good enough, they don't really belong; feelings that can be accentuated knowingly or unknowingly, by default or on purpose by church members themselves. While this at best confuses an understanding of the family of God as an inclusive community, at worst it sends out the message that the criterion used to define membership is man-made and not borne out of the solid principles and values appreciated in a universal understanding of Christ-like values/principles. At the very least, proper recognition needs to be given to the traits and changing circumstances that occur in people's lives and the effect they can have on their personalities, whereby they may lose confidence in themselves, suffer loss of self-esteem, become generally introspective and less sociable and then there is the dreaded outcome of feeling rejected. Alongside them are people known for their learning difficulties and disabilities, for their mental issues, or social impairments. The fact is that all people without distinction can be or are vulnerable for one reason or another, yet not a single person is denied a place in the family of God.

The success of the Wythenshawe churches project work, together with the greater numbers of people being brought together and considered of equal worth, created tension between the church authorities and local church leadership in Wythenshawe over the issue of membership and that was something that became more and more apparent. It was vital to the point of retaining personal integrity that the churches' stance and direction would remain rock solid on the principles and values understood within the concept of the Kingdom of God. To abandon the simple yet profound concept of the universality of the family of

God for what appeared to be no more than institutional church dictate and custom, would have pirouetted and sent hurling away everything the churches became known for through their vision inspired Kingdom, which was constant in their sights.

NORTHENDEN COMMUNITY PROJECTS (NCP)

To say the church was doomed was not an overstatement. 130 years old and still kitted out with its fixed wooden pews, large central pulpit, say nothing of its desperate state of repair it was way past its sell-by-date. When hall and ancillary rooms are added, it became more than apparent that the whole building was fast approaching its terminal end.

Using the Kingdom of God rubric and seizing the initiative to be community project led, the small church community formed a working group with the title Northenden Community Projects (NCP). Following inquiries to local 'service-style' organisations, the National Autistic Society (NAS), a young people's speech and drama organisation, and an existing dancing school, all entered into a partnership with each other and the church. It was a two-part venture; the first part to further develop existing activities whilst at the same time create new initiatives and the second part involved mapping out a new long-term future that might even include a whole new suite of premises. Thus began a closer working relationship among the newly formed partner organisations with meetings to search for a future that would live up to and fulfil NCP's mission statement: "To provide meeting points and facilities to local people, through activities, organisations, community lunches and special events, supported by the church's ministry and prayer."

After a relatively short period of time, a programme of achievable initiatives that didn't require long-term planning and funding was put into place and was soon meeting with success. However the 'investment' type enterprises for a long-term future for church and organisations alike, was heading for years of soul searching and painstaking negotiations, setbacks and eventually to dogged determination. Without the vision that the concept of the Kingdom gave and an enterprising never-give-up frame of mind, the aforesaid years of planning and negotiation could easily have produced a catastrophic negative result, instead of the positive outcome that was finally realised.

Applying Kingdom of God characteristics to strategic planning for the Wythenshawe churches was an entirely new phenomenon. Having decided upon service-led projects that would be initiated and followed through regardless of whether they were church or partner organisations, conforming to Kingdom of God criterion was essential. Such an opportunity arose. For the church to secure a long term future would mean working with a housing association. It would provide units for social housing and at the same time create purpose-built premises for a church café/walk-in centre, a day centre and offices for the local National Autistic Society besides accommodation for other N.C.P. organisations.

Securing such a future with all the benefits a reputable housing association would give is something that is not achieved overnight nor without pains-taking planning and negotiation. After years of detailed planning everything associated with the scheme that included units for social housing, hopes and expectations were dashed and that particular Kingdom proclaimed and envisioned by Christ went back to the drawing board; due to the knock-on effect of the 2008 economic collapse. Back at the drawing board, where the church and partner organisations remained until a new vision emerged.

Even that situation had connotations with the Kingdom of God story told by Jesus about treasure being found by someone in a field and then having to wait until it was possible to purchase the field (Mtt.13:44). Imagine that scenario these days, the longer the waiting time, the greater would be the stress and anxiety to the point of a possible breakdown! Other less discerned attributes associated with the Kingdom needed to come into play and refocus minds; attributes such as faith, trust and confidence.

If securing a long-term future had to remain on hold, visualising and then seizing the initiative for short-term enterprises was considered essential. It was decided to convert the church's youth centre into a day centre for people with autism, develop stronger and where possible practical co-operative relationships among partner organisations and provide regular community lunches. Very soon after the necessary research was complete, the church decided to use money held in a bequest matched by new NAS funds to meet the substantial conversion costs to fit out the new day centre. Under the same programme of work, a new kitchen was built and equipment purchased necessary for the community lunches to get started and all the stops were pulled out to accommodate a new partner organisation namely: Northenden Theatre Company Limited.

With partner organisations in place and developing their schemes of work and with funding streams providing finances for the new projects, a new kitchen was built, equipment bought and the theatre company was very quickly making improvements to the church hall. This co-operation among organisations intensified and the service-led projects or 'ministries', to use another title, began operating with considerable success. The theatre company was able to bring much needed expertise to the table, as well as maximising the use of the premises with four week-long performances a year. The hall doubled up as a theatre, a restaurant, a dancing studio, a venue for Messy Church as well as space for all-purpose activities. As this community spirited momentum grew, so did the numbers of people children and adults, accessing the different facilities and the activities expanded substantially. Later recruits as partner organisations included a chair-based exercise class and a messy church community.

Statistics from an audit of people and children accessing the activities in 2008 show evidence of two factors: 1. The large numbers of people accessing the activities was right across the board and not confined to one or two particular organisations or activities. 2. Numbers were increasing at the same time as the spirit of cooperation and shared 'ownership' among the partner organisations was gaining momentum. A sense of 'ownership' was particularly significant as the church community on their own did not anywhere near have the resources to maintain the premises, and were unable to contemplate a new progressive future.

As well as contributing their own specialist work and activity as part of the overall services to local people and families, the partner organisations also provided an important sense of stability and permanence to both the community spirit and to the maintenance of the premises as a whole. It was just at the time when it seemed all possible avenues to secure a long-term future had been exhausted, when a leading member of the Northenden Players Theatre Club shared an idea he had been thinking about.

Using his architectural experience, he devised a plan whereby the existing premises could be adapted and modernised. This would give modern and purpose-built facilities for all organisations and enable the church to proceed with their ambition to provide something of a walk-in centre. Appreciating that this initially was one person's vision, it included:

- Gutting the interior of the church and building a floor to ceiling partition to create a worship area, thus using a third of the space, the other two thirds of the space to be a community hall with the installation of specialist equipment for the dancing school.
- The old church entrance and lobby would be adapted to house a new kitchen and toilets.
- The new church area would accommodate church services, concerts, meetings and group activities.
- The new community hall would give provision to the dancing school, community lunches, speech and drama, chair-based exercises, messy church plus new organisations.
- The current church hall would be converted into a tiered theatre and the current kitchen and vestry turned into changing rooms.
- The room that used to be a choir room would be an all-purpose meeting room

An internal conversion and modernisation programme such as this would of necessity also require some external structural repair. After presentations, meetings and consultations, the go-ahead was given and funding streams researched. Church funds to the last penny were spent on the structural repairs and confidence was high that applications to funding bodies and trusts for all the interior conversion work and re-build would be successful. The scheme was divided into three parts;

1. the conversion of the church into a worship area, multi-purpose hall and new toilets and kitchen;

2. the conversion of the church hall into a tiered theatre;

3. the conversion of the old church kitchen into a changing room and facility for the theatre.

The go-ahead was given and in no time at all the first part of the development scheme was under way enabling the distant dream of a long-term future for church and organisations spanning many years of failed hopes was reversed and what was one person's vision, was now everyone's golden opportunity. Besides a team of 'workers' who became engaged in this exciting enterprise, considerable credit for this achievement has to go to the architect visionary who saw the future, knew how to get there and took everyone with him. Not only that, but out of this individual's personal and selfless investment, the church had acquired someone with the knowledge and devotion to 'manage' the church's estate responsibly and in the professional manner it required.

Yet again and not surprisingly, the Roman centurion in the story in Luke chapter 7 about his request to Jesus to heal his slave shows an interesting kinship with the architect visionary, except this time the spotlight is on the centurion himself. His personal characteristics were strikingly different from the expected norms. He showed unparalleled compassion towards his slave, he enjoyed a relationship of trust with some of the Jewish elders, the humility he showed towards Jesus was genuine, the quality of the 'character reference' for the centurion conveyed to Jesus by the Jewish elders was outstanding and the God-given authority the centurion saw in Jesus and valued highly was second to none. It is worth appreciating that these excellent attributes were about someone who was not only a non-Jew but a senior Roman officer of the abhorrent occupying military regime and yet so many, including Jesus had absolute respect for him. On the one hand it was because he loved the Jewish people and helped them build their synagogue, but on the other hand it was because of the principles and values he lived by.

The architect visionary was not a member of the church and did not attend church services. That he had a vested interest in the building is true but he loved the church, held a high regard for the people and was fully engaged and supportive towards the whole community and its project work. The architect visionary, not unlike the centurion, conducted his affairs according to his principles and lived out the values he held dear through his leadership and relationships. In these ways both men's integrity is perceived and their spirituality endorsed. Such personal qualities, not least their spirituality, was in fact their interrelationship with Christ's portrait of the Kingdom of God.

As soon as the newly installed kitchen was complete, volunteer chefs, kitchen assistants, table arrangers and waitresses were in place and ready for action. This was preceded with the usual questionnaire survey, publicity and funding applications. Patrons were given a two choice menu and though the targeted clientele was the person living on their own, living in a formal establishment or having packaged meals, all ages of people and families were catered for and welcomed. The average number of meals ranged from 35 to 40 and clients and staff next door from the newly opened day centre for people with autism were particularly welcomed. As time went on and the community lunches became an established part of village life, a strong community spirit and mutual friendship among patrons flourished. Friendships were enjoyed and much pleasure was gained by meeting up with each other regularly and sharing a natural interest in one another's welfare and the usual joys and sorrows life brings.

It is interesting that when the highly successful and much valued church's Women's Bright Hour ceased because of a decreasing membership, the onset of the community lunches could rightly be viewed as more than a replacement. With its inclusive approach, the community lunches brought people together from a wide network of people, offered pastoral care, counsel, hospital visits; all in a sensitive manner as would be appropriate and acceptable. This was serving people in a not dissimilar way to the age-long values of the Women's Bright Hour but doing so more comprehensively, with a wider network of people and with an on-going personal interest in them and in their circumstances. This spirit of friendship and togetherness was also endorsed and reinforced among the community lunch staff, staff from the NAS day centre and teaching staff plus pupils from a local school who occasionally entertained patrons with their repertoire of songs. This shows the wider network of people and personnel who were able to contribute something positive to the common good and likewise, gained something personally from it at the same time.

Lessons learned simply from the community lunch project alone are revealing. The Kingdom of God principles that underpinned the lunches, gave the whole enterprise an authenticity that included everyone who in any way became associated with the lunches. There was not one single source of Christian or spiritual recognition given to the patrons and volunteer staff, but all manner of Christ-like distinguishing hallmarks found their identity in Kingdom of God values. When purposeful consideration is given to the variety of situations encountered by Jesus with the acknowledgement that they were part and parcel of his work and ministry, it is perfectly admissible to appreciate the diverse nature of the Kingdom of God they describe. Likewise, it is not only the community lunches, but the entire work of Northenden Community Projects that was validated by the same principles advocated by Christ himself. These sentiments can be taken a stage further as they purport to show a wider dimension of being a 'church' than conventional or traditional churches assert.

A 'church' so called is not necessarily identified by its place of worship and neither by its membership figures, its congregation, or by a particular message or title, not even through individual conversions. A 'church' seen through the eyes of God's Kingdom can be appreciated in many dimensional forms over and above representation through its congregation. Rather, the 'church' as a community of individuals is wherever the authentic spirit of Christ is evident or is experienced. It was in that appreciation of 'church' with no restrictive elements and an all-inclusive approach in motivation and in practice, which the church at Northenden through its NCP programme of project work and through its network of partner organisations and personnel, became.

The concentration in this last chapter on Northenden Community Projects elucidates the way the different characteristics manifested in church ministry, community enterprise and specialised project work, combined to make a contribution to the common good; but a common good that is at the heart of communities whose ethos epitomised Christ-like values. Similar concentrations can and have been made to the contrasting work of the other churches, as they all featured initiatives with a range of partner organisations and activities.

NEW DAWN – THE BEGINNINGS

In the same way as the other four churches, Lawton Moor church people knew the time had come for a new future, but that future needed a different approach from the way things had been done in the past. It was decided to conduct a major review of the neighbourhood where the church was situated. This involved a research initiative as comprehensive as it could be with as much statistical evidence of the strengths and weaknesses of the local community as possible. Through the auspices of wide ranging questionnaires and contacts with all manner of local services, a feasibility study proceeded and produced very interesting and useful data. Some of the services contacted were health centres, clinics, dentists, schools, social workers, health visitors, councillors and counsellors, probation service, shops, cafes and churches. There were other ways too to measure the strengths and weaknesses of neighbourhood communities and not least among them was word of mouth by neighbours, pub landlords, shop assistants, funeral directors and the like. Analysis of the research revealed where and what the weaknesses were and from a community standpoint, what needed to be addressed. A community Open Day was arranged to which as many as possible personnel from professional community service-led agencies and leaders from voluntary organisations were invited.

A large gathering representing many from the list of organisations and services mentioned above attended and a presentation by the church on the findings of the research was given. Contributions from the assembled company very quickly identified gaps in much needed service-provision and suggested solutions were offered, as well as personal assistance in whatever attempts could remedy the situation.

From the outset, this established the chosen method of future church ministry for all five churches namely: a collaborative approach with organisations and personnel that would form a partnership of complementary services. It was quite a break-through in terms of a body of people from the statutory and professional services and from the voluntary sector too, sharing know-how and finding ways to work together in the interests of the whole neighbourhood.

Whichever way the descriptions and examples of the Kingdom of God in the synoptic gospels (Matthew, Mark and Luke) are read, they all point to a wider audience/clientele and a larger political/social context, than the initial singular subject matter suggests. Likewise, from an analysis of the data and information gleaned from the community research study, it was possible to give serious consideration to the social and spiritual needs of the local people. Similar tasks in the past albeit in different ways, would have been tackled by the church and their service providing organisations in their own right. Having successfully completed the much needed community research and drawn together supporting organisations and clientele, it was pivotal to capitalise on that affiliation by developing personal relationships so that a diverse and effective combined service/ministry could be given.

All this was a result of an Open Review Day which led to the discovery of a new future, new associated colleagues, new potential partner organisations and a vision of the Kingdom of God different from anything in the past. The name of New Dawn was suggested as the title of this initiative because it captured the essence of a new dawn that was beginning to emerge, a new dawn that was universal in its appeal and infinite in its breadth as its mission wording suggests: "The overall aim is to give cradle to grave provision from a place at the hub of its locality with emphasis on family, child and personal support, supported by the church's ministry of worship and prayer."

Besides a reciprocal relationship with organisations which was beneficial to the people we were in the process of serving, there was also a spiritual component that was equally beneficial especially to the church and organisations who became the service providers. The spiritual dimension was most noticeable in the recognition of a common purpose, a shared objective and in mutual support given and received. In some instances this was experienced through what can best be described as perceived awareness, sensing a 'oneness' between service provider and recipient, a sharing of respected values, values that were drawn from a new code of practice. Such spirituality is likewise prominent in the respect given and received by Jesus with those whom he served in a variety of ways. On those occasions, the sense of 'oneness' and 'sharing of values' between Jesus and the people he encountered were very noticeable and due acknowledgement was given to the place of such Kingdom values in the diversity of those relationships.

In the same way, the sense of 'oneness' experienced at this early stage of New Dawn's ascendency was as prophetic as it was tangible and the rummage sales particularly reverberated that solidarity and not least in the context of God's Kingdom. An account of the Rummage Sales is detailed in chapter 5 under the title: The Kingdom of God seen through testimony and solidarity.

This was not the sole prerogative of New Dawn or any of the other project initiatives with partner organisations. Rather, it became a common feature in relationships across the board, just as the Kingdom of God principles became the founding ideals.

NEW DAWN – COUNSELLING SERVICE

One of the partner organisations of New Dawn is New Dawn Counselling. And one of the needs highlighted in the research review was the lack of a professional counselling service and further inquiries confirmed it. Lawton Moor church, where New Dawn was conceived which became the base for the counselling service, was in a part of the housing estate that didn't have the usual community services the other three quarters of the estate enjoyed. That is one reason why a counselling service was nowhere to be seen and neither was there a goodly selection of other services and facilities available. With a plethora of unspoken and none-dealt-with personal issues, it only required one person to volunteer her services for the situation to be addressed. This one volunteer and the minister of the church discussed the situation, at the end of which they both were convinced a counselling service could and should be established.

Although extremely large, the housing estate was reasonably self-contained and in the main, looked out onto urban middle class residential communities which were from a very different cultural background and setting. Counselling services like other personal services operating in the more urban affluent communities were able to charge clients the going rate as they could afford them. If similar rates were charged on the housing estate among a population struggling to make ends meet on a much lower economic budget, they would clearly not be able to afford the fees, be denied a much needed service and inevitably become the poorer emotionally, mentally, socially and even physically as a result. This indeed is what was happening and repeated many times over.

One of the principal reasons why poverty existed and did not appear to decrease was because personal services like counselling and other paid-for service provision simply cost too much. And as the very services tailor-made to improve a person's or a family's circumstances were by, default denied them, the cycle of impoverishment continued and at the same time the underlying issues further compounded their situation. "Where is the justice?" was a term often used by residents and service practitioners alike and the counselling service was just one social programme among many set up to redress that imbalance. The Kingdom of God as taught and lived by Christ was continually redressing imbalances that affected individuals and communities, since the very ideals the Kingdom stood for were for a just way of life for everyone. The counselling service was ranked alongside those same ideals, providing a service available to all people with no strings attached. It was hoped that the counselling would give a positive lead towards healing, wholeness and acceptance, and this indeed is what happened. There are documented many situations in which peoples' lives and circumstances were turned around and unjust situations were made just.

New Dawn Counselling published an annual report which gave comprehensive coverage of their work and working practice including statistical evidence. Besides actual counselling given to recipients, the service assisted the training of counsellors, gave supervision to counsellors, organised sessions for in-service training and was a recognized placement agency for the training of counsellors by Manchester Metropolitan University. It was a free service but accepted donations as and when appropriate. The venue was given free of charge but an annual donation was always given to the church. It had a constituted committee, held regular meetings and gave time for prayer and biblical reflection. It was a member of New Dawn Association and Wythenshawe Oasis as well as being a member of the British Association of Counselling and Psychotherapy and of the Association of Christian Counsellors.

A list of issues or subjects frequently involved in counselling sessions included the following:

- Personal development
- Stress, worry, anxiety
- Depression
- Bereavement, grief and loss
- Relationship problems
- Marriage/family difficulties
- Childhood sexual abuse
- Low self esteem
- Fear
- Spiritual concerns
- Guilt
- Anger
- Inability to cope
- Drug or alcohol addiction
- Sexuality
- Eating disorders
- Money issues
- Housing problems

Such a list detailing so many issues is a reminder of the complexities that are widespread in modern society and the overwhelming need for quality counsellors and counselling. When that counselling is available as part of a compendium of services without bias or favour, its value can be measured against many a personal conversation Jesus entered into with individuals of his day.

(A brief history of New Dawn Counselling has been compiled by the service's founder Andrea Thomas and is available on request from Rev. David Bown)

BROWNLEY GREEN COMMUNITY BAKERY

There are several ways to introduce Brownley Green's Community Bakery project and here are some of them:

- The original kitchen was like something out of the First World War and should have been condemned even before then...!

- The new kitchen and its location is open plan style, accessible to everyone in every situation and is spacious with enough room around the working surfaces for up to ten people at a time...

- Get a whiff of that gorgeous just-out-of-the-oven bread baking smell and you can't resist it...

- The Kingdom of Heaven is like yeast that a woman took and mixed into a large amount of flour until it worked through all the dough...

Anyone who knows anything about the value of yeast to a lump of dough, about bread as being the stable diet, should have a reasonable idea of what it was that Jesus was implying in his parable. He was making the point that it is through the ordinary every-day domestic routines and preoccupations of life, that we can discover important facts that connect us to the Kingdom of God. Having made or acknowledged those facts, it is essential to appreciate their worth in the significance they hold and in the part we enable them to occupy within ourselves.

As a substance of pure quality in its own right, what the yeast gives to the dough, to its proving ability, its baking and to its taste, are the bread's essential ingredients. But something of its innate character would be misplaced or at worse lost if the yeast in its production stage was not evenly distributed through the dough's kneading process. Similarly the yeast wouldn't be able to fulfil its potential or apply its worth as yeast if the dough was not kept at a warm, even temperature. That fact alone draws attention to the yeast's own power, in that it energises the whole dough with multitudes of air pockets and at the same time creates a smooth aerated texture. Another point to cogitate upon is the yeast's ability to give cohesion to the different grains in the flour noticeable particularly in bread made with granary or oatmeal flour. Lastly, the yeast performs best when the associated ingredients flour, salt, sugar, warm water and the non-essential but bonus ingredient of olive oil are mixed evenly together. The complementarity of 'ingredient togetherness' is indispensible.

Whether these ideas were part of Christ's thinking process when he chose yeast to illustrate his teaching on the Kingdom of God is not known. What is known is their usefulness in trying to gain as much insight as possible in the picture Jesus was drawing of the Kingdom itself. The process of dough making was used among the new community bakers at Brownley Green and they too, through their bread making procedure, become an unmistakable part of that Kingdom. To put it simply, yeast expands and multiplies and so does the Kingdom of God.

The former kitchen at Brownley Green, was like something out of the First World War and should have been condemned! Not unlike the other four church properties, Brownley Green's old 'condemned' kitchen was reminiscent of most of the churches' interiors thus illustrating their church communities need of a new purpose, a new ministry, a new vision - in short, a new theology of mission and the community bakery at Brownley Green became an important constituent of that new theology.

The first time a community bakery was even hinted, was during an 'off the-cuff' conversation with someone in the five churches and Wythenshawe Oasis office at St. Andrew's House. Yemi was merely passing by but stayed long enough for a coffee and then entered into an on-going informal conversation about the work at Brownley Green. "Make bread" she said and though it sounds ridiculous, those two simple words very quickly got us talking about a bakery, a community bakery. Yemi was originally from Nigeria and besides being a fellow lay project manager in her own right, she had already started a successful ethnic food co-operative at Brownley Green, so she knew the scene there. The new open-plan kitchen that replaced the 'first world war one' was ideally designed to fit the bill; all that was needed now was the primary objective that would spell out such a community bakery's selling points. A visit to a community bakery in Liverpool that was already well established and proving to be a most effective and impressive project, helped the Brownley Green contingent to spell out the selling points for their own bakery. And so the overall aims and objectives became thus:

1. Create an environment at Brownley Green that would be a mutual meeting point for people who are engaged in the same programme of activity.

2. Enable the programmed activities to facilitate a setting conducive to the needs of a therapeutic community.

3. Give as much help to the participators as required so that they feel properly valued among fellow compatriots within a 'giving and receiving' ethos.

4. Provide the 'tools' and the assistance that will enable every participator to have that importance sense of achievement.

5. Nurture a spirit of community the impact of which will encourage the participators to come back and re-establish their relationships with fellow 'bakers'.

The logistics of the enterprise meant some basic equipment was required included a replacement cooker, a dough prover and a dough machine, though the latter was not a necessity at that stage. Smaller items were mixings bowls, jugs, chopping boards and general miscellaneous kitchen/bakery utensils and these were funded through Wythenshawe Oasis.

From these beginnings an overall vision of the project became much clearer and it was this:

(a) People from the local neighbourhood, people drawn from the world of disabilities and impairments and people with their own groups and gatherings would be encouraged to come along to the community bakery and make bread.

(b) Special attention would be given to people who would particularly value and gain much from the 'community spirit' the 3-hour bread making experience would give them and these included the high proportion of one parent adults, adults with low self-esteem and individuals who think they are skill-less and non-achievers.

(c) Children facilities would be provided with specialised equipment and competent supervision which would enable single parents the same access as anyone. The play facilities were organised and made operational through the assistance of Wythenshawe Oasis.

(d) For the long-term, the community bakery would have the resources to develop further the enterprise and establish a community café with the products for buying and eating being made on the premises as an extension of the bread making.

(e) The end result should be many mini therapeutic communities as each group takes their places around the kitchen working surface and meet individual needs amid first-time achievements in the discovery of skills long hidden. The living out of the church's mission aims and making real in contemporary society the hidden message and meaning of the 'yeast' parable told by Jesus, was one way the kingdom of heaven found favour among the 'bakers' and people at Brownley Green.

With resources in place, the community bakery began rolling out bread - two loaves per participating baker, one to keep and one to give away. Each session catered for up to ten participants standing either side of the low level working surface. Everyone went through the bread making process in unison, weighing the ingredients, making and kneading the dough, moulding and placing it on the baking tray or in the bread tin and leaving it to prove until it was ready for baking. The waiting period during proving was a good opportunity to tidy up and enjoy homemade soup provided by one or more of the participants. During the half hour baking period, the time was usefully used catching up on each other's news and general socialising. There is no doubt about the good and excited experience enjoyed by the vast majority of participants culminating in the thrill of their two loaves of bread which always drew wide-spread smiles of pride. At the same time, the value of the unseen, unpretentious dynamics of a therapeutic community in its most natural setting was social and spiritual health care at its best.

Having done the research and pieced together the whole project like a jigsaw, the vital element was the theology that underpinned it. By 'theology' I mean where the purposes of God fit into the jigsaw. In other words; where and how the values and principles of God's Kingdom were conceived as essential elements featured in every part of the project's construction. Just as this was fundamental to all the project work and activities; so too were the 'theological' or biblical contributions coming as they did from the raft of Christ's teaching. To name in this instance just one component that illustrates this technique, it is found in Matthew 13:33:

"The Kingdom of Heaven is like yeast that a woman took and mixed into a large amount of flour until it worked through all the dough." That short twenty-six word sentence became a profound statement that was acted out at Brownley Green time and time again as a living parable, except the yeast invaluable as it was in the production of the two loaves of bread, was in this community setting the participating bakers themselves! Appreciating the dynamic working potential of the yeast as expounded in the 3rd paragraph, when that yeast concept is transferred onto the people and they as it were become the product ie: the yeast of the leaven. It should not be surprising that the ethos it creates, has a distinguishing feature likened to a people and atmosphere at a communion service and you need look no further in your search for the Kingdom of Heaven or Kingdom of God. But in order to seek and find that precious Kingdom people, required nothing less than overturning that antiquated pre-war condemned kitchen and working through everything else that eventually led to the new community bakery. And though the kingdom people became the precious reality, it was only when every individual piece of that community bakery project jigsaw was carefully matched up and assembled together, could the Kingdom of God be truly seen and appreciated throughout the whole of the operation.

It is the contention of this dissertation that the tried and tested Kingdom of God approach by Christ himself, provides not only the best foundation for mission work, but it alone gives integrity to the local church, integrity to mission initiatives and activities, integrity to sister and brother in Christ relationships and above all, makes absolute sense of the real and actual value embedded in the meaning of the Kingdom of God today.

When relationships of the sincerity outlined above happen especially with people from a diverse and those from a disadvantaged background, the Kingdom of Heaven which is 'like yeast a woman took and mixed into a large amount of flour' story, ceases to be merely something from the past and becomes a dynamic contemporary reality. But remember - not only the transforming effect of the yeast, important though that is, but it's phenomenal transference, its incarnation in the people themselves, who become Kingdom people without any ceremony or ecclesiastical identity or membership. It is they who are also the church, the church in their own right.

Statements such as these are not subjective quibbles but an objective observation and analysis. Anyone can be pre judged and judged wrongly simply by living on a housing estate especially when that housing estate is Wythenshawe, with all its notoriety and where prejudice and disfavour are singled out without trying. This all too frequently leads to categorising people as being somehow less significant than others, especially from those of a different background or class of society. When this happens, it is a totally wrong way to acknowledge a person's existence and can cloud, obliterate even the uniqueness of someone's personal gifts and graces; let alone reveal any positives embedded within their personality. Placing Kingdom of God values alongside people enables the worth of everyone to be seen, to be acknowledged and to be appreciated.

THE NATIONAL AUTISTIC SOCIETY, SIGNPOST & MESSY CHURCH

"Our service is open to anyone with a diagnosis of autism and as our programmes are flexible and tailored to what each person needs and wants, people can choose the centre which best meets their needs. Through our services, we give adults with autism the chance to learn and try new experiences by offering a wide range of groups, classes and activities, allowing people to follow their interests and develop their life skills and knowledge in a meaningful way."

"The Young People Support Foundation (YPSF) but known locally at St. Andrew's as Signpost, provides a wide range of services to support young people towards an independent life as an adult. Our services range from practical support and advice for those at immediate risk of homelessness, to help with learning how to find employment, cook healthy meals or budget for household bills."

These two statements are from organisations that formed partner relationships with their churches and the equal-ness of those relationships is seen in two ways, as an investment and as a ministry. The investment was the commitment to oversee and cover the costs of major interior refurbishment programmes in the two church buildings; and the new ministries was the practical work among people with autism and work with young adults particularly those who were potentially at risk.

The major refurbishment by The National Autistic Society adding considerable investment value was matched by the significant contribution Signpost undertook as part of a major interior re-design of their work space at St.

Andrew's church. Further mention of Signpost's 'ministry' work is given in chapter 5.

These refurbishment initiatives by the NAS and Signpost meant the church buildings would by necessity be upgraded, and the seriously over-due repairs and defects would at long last be put right, as well as securing a long-term future and pleasing premises for a professional work environment. Most important of all, it meant securing a ministry of pastoral care and specialised work among local people that would have been beyond the churches to deliver. At the same time the churches and partner organisations knew that the most important aspect of their existence was the delivery of the services or ministries they were commissioned to undertake.

A third organisation that features in this section is Messy Church based at Northenden and all three organisations as will be seen, are serious about their aims and objectives. When their mission statements are held up to the light or personally checked out, all three organisations are found to be 'not far from the Kingdom of God' as in the statement made by Jesus concluding his dialogue with the teacher of the law (Mark 12:34). So a brief look at the principal work offered by the NAS, Signpost and Messy Church are of considerable interest and enlightenment.

The church's commitment to people with autism, through its relationship with the NAS, involving the use of a substantial sum of money from a bequeathed fund to part finance premises for people with autism, was an act of unquestioned generosity. Likewise the NAS also made a sizeable contribution towards the costs to convert the church's redundant youth centre into a day centre primarily for people with autism. Such was the strength of the partner relationship with the local NAS that the church was able to play its part in offering the public a much needed provision with all its essential service-led specialism.

"We want every adult we support to have the opportunity to develop and thrive and to be at the centre of his/her planning process. We work closely with people to create their individual plan and support them to keep it live. Through our knowledge and experience we enable people to communicate effectively and to express their wishes. We also make sure that family, carers, friends and staff are full partners in the planning process." (Taken from the mission statement of the NAS)

The NAS, through the new Day Centre at Northenden, is serving a very special clientele most effectively and at the same time playing a vital role as part of the Northenden Community Projects the church and other partners are committed to. The NAS was the first organisation to create a partnership with the church and in time gave important stimulus to the whole church project at Northenden which was vital when considering the 'wilderness' years the NCP team had to plough through, before it was able to truly seize the initiative and go for its vision.

Likewise, the value of Signpost to its church of St. Andrew's is best appreciated as an evolving development, both in terms of the modernisation of the space it occupied which was half the premises of a moderate to large size church. In terms of the social ambience its conferencing activities and every-day human presence resonated around the building. The modernisation programme turned a suite of premises that had far exceeded their sell-by date into purpose-built accommodation including spacious office bases, interview rooms, a coffee bar-cum breakfast common room and a well equipped kitchen, all of which are accessed from an attractive corridor and a welcoming entrance foyer and reception. Positioned facing the car park and the drive leading out to the main road, Signpost were always on hand to receive callers and visitors and direct them to their respective designation. I have always appreciated this service from Signpost especially for the purposes of receiving contractors and commercial personnel; and many a time Signpost has dealt with the business concerning these and other representatives and callers on my behalf.

Another valuable input by Signpost has been their involvement with other partner organisations at the New Horizons project meetings. Recurring matters for action have included day-time security as well as outside security lights, every-day cleaning of the toilets, emergency property repairs and an on-going consultation on an increasingly leaking roof! A new roof was eventually built on the Hall at the same time as a new church roof, owing to the theft of a considerable proportion of its original copper tiling. Sorting these necessities out through a collective approach meant all organisations shared the responsibility but as Signpost's needs were more acute, their participation in dealing with maintenance concerns was much more a shared undertaking with me and one that was valued very highly. Such a shared approach even extended in some instances to joint funding arrangements whereby we would submit funding bids for repairs and renewals to the premises and at the same time as funding for Signpost's own enterprises and initiatives. It was in these ways too, the entire premises internally and externally were kept in good repair including the grounds and even the dear old flower beds!

Operating, as Signpost does primarily with young people aged 16-25 but not excluding 14 and 15 year olds when needs necessitate it, is what it does best and why Signpost is at St. Andrew's. Some young people under its care and supervision live with parents or relatives. Some are in council care while yet others could most likely be sleeping rough. It matters not, whether the young people are single, part of a couple relationship or have children. "If we can't provide the help you need" it teaches, "we'll be able to supply you with the details of someone who can; and any young person can ask for help no matter what their background, race, religion, sexual orientation, history or health status is or implies. All our services are free and confidential." Something of that all-round comprehensive service is symbolised in a machine that clearly caught my attention the first time I noticed it and made me think to myself; "That's the first time I have seen a condom slot machine as a wall fixture in a corridor of a church building!" But at the same time, I have been pleased and felt re-assured on those occasions I have referred young people and adults to talk with staff at Signpost; and have benefitted in my work from briefings and advice Signpost staff have given me.

When Messy Church opened its doors for the first time at Northenden it was not greeted by the church congregation with a great fanfare of delight and optimism, which was disappointing to say the least. No matter how much explanation and insight is given into the workings of a Messy Church, sometimes it seems the approach towards children's work and methods is just too different from traditional Sunday Schools which the older church population especially know best. Nevertheless, Messy Church at Northenden has been a pioneering movement that has clearly established itself for the very reasons the initiative was first launched. The Messy Church programme involves toddlers with their mums or dads, grandparents or carers and children of primary school age in particular, and being introduced to a range of activities most of which are made and crafted with their hands. These are set out on tables positioned around the hall and follow a particular sequence. The activities don't have to be done in a specific order except that by the time you come to the last table the hand-made object appears in its completed form. There are sometimes other more physical type activities also and all of them together play their part in developing the biblical story or theme that is being explored. All this is preceded with a cooked breakfast usually comprising sausages of one kind or another or a vegetarian option; with of course squash and a choice of tea or coffee, though it can be as simple as fruit juice and cake, savouries, or whatever individual Messy Churches wish to provide. The last session comprises a circle often with the smallest children in the front and adults at the back and consists of lighted candles, the Bible story either being told as a story or is acted out, some singing, participatory prayers - and all within a spiritual setting of oneness and sincere devotion to God. It hardly requires spelling out! The whole purpose and setting is carefully put in place to draw maximum spontaneity and participation from everyone; and the informal/relaxed friendly environment enhances and helps make the overall theme an actual experience and not just something that has been learned. People and families are drawn to Messy Church principally from the Northenden area which makes the project neighbourhood based, whilst at the same time creating a real sense of community in its own right from its all-age participants. To enormous credit, that is precisely what Messy Church at Northenden achieves.

Something happened one particular Sunday morning which had a positive effect on Messy Church as well as receiving important recognition. A child of one of the families was to be baptised and the question arose whether the baptism should or would take place within the usual setting of messy church, or whether the baptism would take place as part of the church's usual Sunday morning worship. The parents of the child conducted their own straw poll among Messy Church clientele and families and decided the baptism would be held in church as part of the Sunday Service. This is how one eye witness on the occasion itself described what happened...

"The church was full of family, friends and the regular congregation and they all mixed in together. David, the preacher, began his sermon with a picture, a special picture in fact that was drawn by someone from the group of artists based at Studio One over at St. Andrew's church. Using that particular drawing which showed an unnamed child's features, David began his story about the boy with the five loaves and the two fish at the feeding of the five thousand at the same time engaging the congregation, asking questions and allowing free movement of the children in church as their attentions peaked and ebbed. This led into making loaves of bread using pre-made bread dough."

"You could see the congregation looking at each other and wondering what was happening at such an unusual service, but they were all soon immersed in making their five loaves, as in the story, while still sat at their pews; conversation flowed and everyone helped each other. Children delivered the materials to all members of the congregation and the atmosphere buzzed. Everyone ended up with a box of five loaves to bake at home. The story continued by David explaining who the boy in the picture drawn by the said artist could be, linking it to the child getting baptised and the qualities he would hopefully grow up to have, similar to the boy with the loaves and fish. The regular congregation joined in happily with the more interactive parts of the service; engaged with practical activities and conversation. The songs and singing were also a mixture of traditional and modern."

"I ask myself, what all-round impact did the service make if any? The baptism is well remembered among family even years later and they seemed to enjoy the service much more than usual baptisms. They went home and were contacting me that evening saying how they had enjoyed the service and how their bread rolls had come out after baking. I feel it gave a more rounded service, meeting the collective needs of the congregation, while providing all the elements of a traditional service." So said the parents of the boy who was baptised.

Due to the attendance of messy church people, the congregation was more than twice its usual size. The service to a large extent followed a similar pattern and style to Messy Church. The baptism liturgy (order of service) was composed (written) expressly for the occasion. The Sunday morning congregation were for the first time introduced to a messy church format and experience. All the Sunday church people were together as one body and no less as, One Body of Christ. Was this a turning point for the church congregation and for Messy Church? Was recognition given to Messy Church that wasn't noticeable before? What all-round impact if any was made? Let the founder of Northenden Messy Church and her husband speak for themselves...

"Was this a turning point for the congregation and for messy church? Was recognition given to Messy Church, which wasn't given before? I am not sure if the regular congregation understood that the alternative service had a Messy Church structure to it. I feel if there were more alternative services like this, because they are so enjoyable they would be accepted more and maybe the regular congregation would begin to integrate into Messy Church services as well."

There are particular insights to be drawn from these examples of integrated working relationships and shared ministry. In their own unique way, all three of these organisations fulfil a most important role in the work of the Kingdom of God.

The National Autistic Society at Northenden through their specialist work with adults with autism and their offer of a ministry of grace, well-being and personal care; giving dignity and a sense of worth that can be considered a form of healing to individuals with complex needs.

Signpost is a light of hope to the younger generation and offers role models as well as helping individuals to respect society as much as they can/should respect themselves; as well as being the light at the end of the tunnel.

Messy Church at Northenden enables families and their children a rare opportunity to 'experience' the Christian Faith by making the biblical passages creatively adventurous, showing an allegiance and a responsibility to the world in a way that is true and spiritual; and by enjoying the relationships of those around them as well as that of the unseen Christ.

Without these three organisations, the work of the Kingdom of God in and outside their respective church's, would be severely reduced as too would the administration and maintenance of the churches be made far more difficult. The important sense of colleagueship and comradeship, of sharing God-given talents for the common good and of being a rich spiritual resource, besides a source of priceless encouragement, is like "the Kingdom of Heaven when a landowner who went out early in the morning to hire men to work in his vineyard..." (Matthew 20:1) And one of the messages Jesus was highlighting in this parable of the Workers in the Vineyard, was the realisation that in God's eyes, all people are of equal worth and equal value irrespective of circumstance, background or personal hardship. These three and their associated organisations clearly demonstrated the truth of that declaration with immense verve, blessing and spiritual grace.

ANECDOTES:

Posh dinner at Altrincham

Early into our new and ambitious project work, and to show genuine value and respect to church folk of all five churches and associates, myself and the team made up from representatives of our churches organised a formal-like dinner for everyone. Held at nearby Altrincham Methodist Church, we numbered 150 give or take a few. For us, this required careful planning and organisation because it was most important that everyone was accommodated. It could have heralded a new and adventurous beginning and I suppose that critical factor without making it obvious, was apparent. The true purpose of the event however, was to show real appreciation and respect to a people upon whom our corporate vision hung, for if we were going to place great value and resolution on our Kingdom of God work, we first needed to acknowledge the value we were to each other. The evening was a defining moment in the history and in the future of the churches, a special occasion in every way as the intervening years bore out.

Studio One & the chicken

An early call one day at St. Andrew's House asked if I knew a chicken had been found half buried in a window box outside Studio One. Because the manager of Studio One had quite a wit with a humour to match, we soon embarked upon a frivolous and jokey conversation about the things you could do when you find a dead chicken! All became more serious tone when the manager's colleague arrived and insisted burying the hen appropriately in the garden at St. Andrew's House. That left us unravelling the mystery of how a dead chicken could be half buried in a window box. We concluded that a fox would hardly go to all that trouble in an attempt to cover his tracks, any more than the hen's sisters would be able to half bury her either! It so happened that the previous evening's occupants in the church was a large African congregation and not really suspecting them of any mal practice, I knew they had to be approached in case they could throw any light on the quandary. Tried as I did when talking to their church official that they were not prime suspects in some sort of ritual ceremony, the protestations that were released obviously made them feel vulnerable. The mystery was never solved, but what became apparent was the importance of a close working relationship especially with organisations whom by the nature of their work, operate in a surrounding ethos of vulnerability.

Trust, respect and confidence in each other are essential qualities for cooperative working relationships as the principals embedded in the Kingdom of God declare and New Horizons organisations were never slow living them out.

The buggy at Dunham Massey

What a sight and absolutely typical! This is in reference to 'outrageous behaviour' by half a dozen characters from Brownly Green church; they were the volunteer workers of 'Mo's Cabin' charity shop. Folk from all five churches and projects were on a day's outing to Dunham Massey, an old Georgian house and gardens with lakes and wild fowl on an estate run by The National Trust. After an extensive picnic with reminders of the feeding of the five thousand and while everyone was enjoying the different features of the place, one of those electric passenger carrying buggies you see at airports, went quietly by save for one thing; the passengers in it! They were Mo's lot from Brownley Green making a right old din as they laughed, shouted and waved their arms about like school children being released from class lessons. But instead of it being outrageous behaviour, it was a sight to behold, abandoned 'respectability' to be sure and a joy that captivated the spirit of the day as well as the exuberant personalities it portrayed.

CHAPTER 4:
THE KINGDOM OF GOD SEEN THROUGH TESTIMONY AND SOLIDARITY

T his chapter takes us to all five churches and to a wide variety of project work where each activity has its own distinctive purpose, yet in solidarity with each other. They stand as testimonials to their character and service to the common good.

Commonality and Solidarity

HEALTHY LIVING NETWORK

Leave to one side the Levite and the priest in the story of the Good Samaritan and concentrate on the injured man left to die and the Samaritan who came to his aid as the principal characters. If no-one had attended to the injured man, he would have died and would have been just another statistic alongside all the others who had met a similar cruel and vicious death. No-one would have been any the wiser and no positive message for public interest would have been gleaned from that tragic event. It is not known whether in telling that story Jesus was using actual evidence from a real-life situation, or whether it was one of his skilfully-pictured fictitious narratives. Either way it would have captured the imagination and the outrage of his hearers; and left ringing in their ears the essential message he had wanted and hoped they would hear. No-one irrespective of their race, culture, religion, status, life-style or circumstances should be left unattended and uncared-for regardless of the prevailing situation with all its ensuing dangers and life-threatening risks. That's the first part of the message. The second part is centred round the Samaritan, the person who exercised 'agape' love. He alone who, culturally, politically and historically was the injured man's enemy, bandaged him up and attended to more than his basic health needs by taking him to a safe-from-harm hostelry and making sure his future welfare needs were met in full.

Baguley Hall Church, one of the five Wythenshawe Methodist Churches, named its project the Harvest Centre, it's mission statement read: "To provide an all-age range of activities, therapies and care with emphasis on healthy living and easy learning especially for the over 50s, supported by the church's ministry of worship and prayer." But that church's initial road to a future ministry of health and welfare for the over 50s especially, took a circuitous route with reminders of that Jerusalem to Jericho road the injured man and the Samaritan were travelling down.

In the name of the Harvest Centre and with Methodist Homes as its partner organisation, detailed research and plans had been carried out to build a residential home for elderly people that would occupy space around and on the site of the church. The land was owned by Manchester Methodist Housing Association who were party to the negotiations, but at the eleventh hour and without warning they pulled the plug on the project. They would neither sell nor lease the land to either Baguley Hall Church or Methodist Homes. With that particular project's hopes shattered, Baguley Hall church returned to their mission statement and conceived an entirely new scheme whereby they could still provide the healthy living and easy learning package they had committed themselves to. After all the usual feasibility work, planning, contacting key individuals and raising funds, the list of activities and services to the over 50s especially, began to look like this:

- A range of activities under the umbrella name of Healthy Living including: craft work, meditation, exercise, massage, blood pressure tests and advice.

- Specialised sessions to help prevent strokes occurring and give professional support to stroke victims.

- A range of holistic therapies including aroma-therapy and reflexology.

- Computer and I.T. classes with emphasis on word processing, emailing and photography.
- Knitting, stitching and embroidery.
- A satellite (regional) office for Healthy Living Network as part of the local Primary Care Trust's work in a particular part of Wythenshawe.
- Informal semi-worship style meetings for spiritual stimulation and fellowship.
- The Garden of Tranquillity for quiet repose, refreshments and enjoyment.

Nigar Sadique (later to become Franklin) in the role of the Good Samaritan and speaking for herself said, "I underwent extensive research to define areas in Wythenshawe where the most need was in terms of improvement in peoples' health. This resulted in the need to set up various programmes and classes that would help educate people towards a better and more consistent healthy living life-style. I needed to network with organisations to deliver these programmes and then develop activities as well as organise events that could promote public awareness. I had to establish partner relationships with organisations and find places and venues to house them, negotiate low rents as well as provide fees and expenses to voluntary participating organisations. This was all part and parcel of my role as overseer, manager, co-ordinator of Healthy Living Network programmes with and for communities in most need."

"It was in 2002 through contacts with a range of churches and centres that I came into contact with the five Wythenshawe Methodist churches and found them to be most responsive and willing to offer accommodation at low rents. In time my contact with the churches was through Wythenshawe Oasis which began a pro-active period of community development which facilitated a variety of events with various groups and organisations. It was through W.O. that I found my way to the Harvest Centre where they were keen to engage with the more elderly people of the area and provide services tailor-made to their needs. Through my Healthy Living Network (HLN) office I negotiated the setting up of a project at the Harvest Centre aimed to help stroke awareness and preventative measures with Wythenshawe Hospital. This project, which ran three days a week, became very successful. We knew this was going to achieve high results because of the feasibility study we undertook and the high percentage of stroke victims in that particular neighbourhood ascertained through the study. In these and many ways HLN represents local people and their needs at stakeholders meetings as we did at the Harvest Centre. The working relationships with the Methodist churches as with the Harvest Centre at the Baguley Hall Church, were very community orientated and mutually beneficial to both HLN and to WO."

Just as the Samaritan became the saving grace to the Jericho Road man injured and left helpless, so Nigar with her HLN enterprise exercised a similar role towards the Harvest Centre, which quickly became a venue like the hostelry in that story - a place of help, friendship and support in the care of people and the issues facing them in older age. With the exciting, extravagant perhaps, plans to build a residential home scuppered and the small band of church pioneers left with the feelings of anti-climax and lost euphoria, a new idea was tabled and helped enormously by the 'secular' (not dissimilar to the status of the Samaritan) backing of HLN and its entrepreneur manager in the person of Nigar. Her relationship and that of HLN to the Methodist churches is well documented in the answers given in her Wythenshawe Questionnaire she was asked to fill in, a summary of which reads like this:

- "As a partner organisation, HLN worked on a co-equal footing with the churches and me and all my staff were enthusiastic and very supportive and yes, we were a key player, an enabler and co-ordinator around which the churches and other organisations gained encouragement, resources and volunteers."

- "Besides the healthy living activities we did a range of other activities assisted by WO and church volunteers in different venues at different times and these included cooking workshops, chair-based exercises, dancing and a host of educational programmes, they were great fun and hugely successful."

- "How did I see the minister's role? He developed community projects with church, HLN and other organisations and the working relationship was always on a professional footing."

- "What did I think the churches spiritual values were? Making connections with communities and making them feel welcome in the churches especially among vulnerable isolated people and the fact there were never any problems using church space and premises."

- "Did I hear at any time the phrase 'the Kingdom of God'? Yes it was used and it resonated with me as I am also a person of faith, though not of the

Christian Faith. A religious input was noticeable in the way we all worked together as one team and in the way we appreciated the spiritual-ness of everything."

- "The positives in my working relationships with WO, has been in the way we pioneered new initiatives especially the office base that was set up at the Harvest Centre and the funding we provided to pay the trainers for the Harvest Centre's healthy living activities and to get the computer classes off the ground."

- "The negatives? They are so few; I can only think that sometimes I wasn't always sure who the church contact person was."

- "Is there more that could still be achieved? Definitely yes especially now with financial cut-backs and a reduced staff and therefore increased workload, which means we need partner organisations all the more because the needs are always out there."

- "How would I describe the philosophical background to our work? We work in diverse communities around public health issues to improve personal well-being. We introduce people to neighbours and believe in all-round relationships including partnerships with organisations and good colleagueship with one another so that we work as one team."

The questionnaire referred, are known as The Wythenshawe Questionnaire. They were used with partner organisations to ascertain their involvement and participation in the theological and spiritual context of their organisation's work. The completed questionnaires are recorded and produced in different formats; some are re-produced in full while others are integrated in the appropriate text representing that particular organisation's work. Feedback from the first questionnaire is from the manager of South Manchester Healthy Living Network and due to her conversational style with extended commentaries, her answers are written up in the form of a dialogue with me; whilst other questionnaires were completed in a more theoretical / formal style.

BROWNLEY GREEN COMMUNITY DAY

The reason why so many people had come together to form nothing short of a mass crowd in the story of the feeding of the five thousand, was not because they were hungry and neither would it have been the case that every single person was determined to follow Jesus and go wherever he was going. It was most likely due to group solidarity, something as straightforward as that. Albert Nolan is a writer of theology and in his book called 'Jesus before Christianity' he speaks of the seriousness the Jews invested the idea of group solidarity. In reference to Jewish society he says, "Not only were all members of the family regarded as brothers, sisters, mothers and fathers to one another, but they identified themselves with one another. The harm done to one member of the family was felt by all." And he goes on to explain that solidarity was even extended to include one's friends, co-workers and traders, one's social group and even in elitist sects like the Pharisees or the Essenes. Individualism, as in doing things on your own or preferring your own company was unknown, except when saying your prayers. It is hardly surprising therefore that the words of Jesus when in Mark 3:34: "Here are my mother and my brothers, whoever does the will of my Father in heaven is my brother, and sister, and mother," carries in its embrace the whole meaning of group solidarity. No wonder there was not even the slightest hint from Jesus to send the hordes away, despite the fact they had gate-crashed the party and the fact that Jesus and his friends had gone there to be on their own! Instead, as the discussion over what they were going to eat was deepening, the instruction from Jesus was given. If the outcome was one big communal sharing of everyone's lunch-boxes, makes absolute sense of Jewish society's concept of group solidarity and drives home its time honoured status, its rich meaning and its heartfelt value.

Not exactly five thousand, but a huge gathering of people and families of all ages from the entire neighbourhood gave the occasion a semblance of the story of the feeding of the five thousand. This was a fun day, an open day, a carnival day at Brownley Green and everyone was there. The fitness fanatics from the gym, the shoppers from the community shop, the martial art stick fighters, the street dancers, Irish dancers, Morris Dancers, the budding recording artistes, the Sunday congregation, the mums & tots, the sport therapy practitioners, the credit union people, associated organisations as well as lots of families from around the neighbourhood. It was a sight and a site to behold, the Irish and the Street dancers were performing while the Morris Dancers were waiting their turn, the shop's open air stalls were loaded with clothes and nick-knacks, the gym folk were competing to find the strongest man, the grassed area was like one end of a football pitch, music complementing the dancing was blasting forth and in-between times you could hear the unmistakable rhythm of the steel band. All this on a glorious summer's day with people, push-chairs, dogs all milling around while the arousing spicy aromas from the barbecues kept everyone well-nourished and the place full of community spirit and family fun.

This was one of those occasions which had lots of similarities with other community and church events, but it was distinctly different too, so different you were able to perceive something extraordinary about the day. Its extraordinariness was due to a number of factors and not least among them was the spirit of the occasion and this can best be described in the form of a very noticeable spiritual atmosphere, so much so that it dominated the occasion and its stimulus made for some very interesting propositions, they are listed here 1 to 7:

1. A celebratory community event itself can through its own natural friendly character create an atmosphere that will be spiritual in nature and convivial in expression and there was no exception to that on this occasion.

2. A spiritual dimension is usually discernible through the positive engagement of the people and their relationship with each other at most organisations' regular meetings. So, when an event like this took place, they all came together in one combined effort and the spiritual contribution from the participating organisations themselves, played a more than significant part in the overall atmosphere the occasion generated.

3. Another form of spiritual input of measureable quality was the spirited and exuberant joy that flooded the place, from the euphoria of the dancers, the exhibitionism in finding the strongest man and in the hale and heartiness of the stall holders, to the five-a-siders, the clusters of picnic-makers and the linked arm friends in their carefree-ness as they strode along in step with each other. Whichever way you looked there was solidarity and harmony in all the pairs and groupings of people whether they were volunteer organisers, members of clubs and groups or the vast numbers of local people from the near-by houses; all of them were of one accord and all of them contributed to and became part of the spirit of the occasion.

4. Last but not least among the many who played their part in spiritual and purposeful ways were the individual people who came from many backgrounds, and extraordinary and difficult circumstances. So many individual people with their own tragic stories, their own behavioural problems, personality issues and unmentionable needs. And whether it's through persistent keep-going-ness or through tried and tested ways to cope, or through finding the means by which they hang-in-there and come what may remain positive, the contribution by them to the overall spiritual atmosphere was as substantial as it was authentic.

5. According to the brevity of the text, the boy who produced the five loaves and two fish in the story of the feeding of the five thousand was just a lad, presumably like others of his age and yet his gift of food resulted in a spiritual awakening. And if indeed such an innocent offering inspired others to share theirs to the extent of basketfuls of food left over, that too can be considered a very human thing to do was in fact something very spiritual too. It is not necessary to spend endless hours in a state of prayer, or being contritely pious or overtly generous, or the poor to be spiritual or spiritually led. Given the appropriate circumstance, your own humanity can in itself produce spiritual worth of such quality and substance, as to make all the difference to a community fun day as it did at Brownley Green.

6. The occasion was a 'once-in-a-while' event and meeting point for everyone and everyone's individual spirit plus the spirit embedded in the ethos of the groups represented, played a very important part in creating a distinct communal hall-mark. It was nothing less than a spiritual community identity made up from individuals and singular communal activities not unlike an imaginary Celtic knot. The Celtic knot is a good description because it appears as an endless cord that weaves in and out of itself to produce interlaced patterns. In the same way the ethos and spirit of the families and organisations, usually separate from each other, were now all joined up in one cohesive mass and the interaction and activities of the people, organisations and groups was like an explosion of collective enthusiasm and celebratory togetherness.

7. One of the most important and fascinating aspects of the Brownley Green story is the vision upon which the church's gym became a reality. The conversion of the church (ie: the worshipping space of the building) to a fully functional gym was the forerunner of the other four churches' project work; it even pre-dated applying the Kingdom of God concept itself in January 1999. Sunday worship had long moved to a different part of the building leaving the original 'church' space redundant and falling into disrepair. The whole concept of the building of the gym was the brain-child of Greg Davis a life-long church member at Brownley Green since his baptism at a few weeks old. Greg knew everything there is to know about Wythenshawe's housing estate - its ups and downs, its good and bad sides, its deep-rooted troubles involving drugs and gang warfare not to mention social deprivation, dysfunctional families and their never ending consequences. His vision was to re-establish in an entirely new (even controversial) way, an environment for Christian witness that would stand for everything the old pulpit and font stood for in their day, except the gym would do it through this modern, innovative and radical initiative. It was a bold courageous undertaking, especially appreciating the vulnerability and the chaos of the estate's fragile social infrastructure. It is well known and documented that it is only an extremely small minority of new 'business enterprises' on housing estates that become successful and Brownley Green is situated at the heart of one of the toughest places on the estate. The vision underpinning the gym initiative was not only a bold undertaking, it was nothing less than prophetic because it not only fulfilled its own objectives, it also found its raison d'etre - its reason for being which astonishingly encapsulated, the Kingdom of God ideological foundation that became the pioneering work of all the five churches.

Let us focus on the gym a little more because it not only reveals outreach mission work in its own right, but it represents much of the project work by the partner organisations of all the churches. The familiar stages from planning to completion required: a feasibility study, a business plan, drawings of the new gym, raising the funds, building and equipping the gym and at the same time rectifying structural faults and promoting the new facility. Two thirds of the floor space gym, the remaining third became an entrance lobby with a reception, a small café area, a games room and a changing room. A mezzanine level was built creating a second floor for running machines, plus rooms for an office and for sports therapy treatment. It is after all this painstaking preparatory work thus described, that the tangible aspects of the Kingdom of God became operative and ever more noticeable and this applied equally to the gym as it did to the other organisations that became established. These noticeable Kingdom of God aspects included:

- A free and easy-going ethos with no swearing or bad language.
- A friendliness that extended to non-gym or fitness activists.
- A café area that welcomed anyone and everyone who wandered in, to stay all day if they wanted to.
- A 'street-wise' venue for characters that are viewed suspiciously or dubiously.
- A welcome environment for young and older adults that have been through the courts.
- A very acceptable meeting point for peer-group socialising.
- A safe place among friends for people with mental health issues.
- A place known and respected for its churchy history and Christian presence.
- A refuge for people facing hardship and a listening ear for people with problems.
- A base and co-ordinating role with partner organisations especially the community shop.
- An every-day presence that oversees maintenance of the grounds, including security of the whole premises.
- A rendezvous for associated organisations, especially the distribution of food products.
- Limitless opportunities to talk to the minister and other caring Christian people.

Many churches let their premises to organisations that hire room space for their activities, but very few enter into an official contract or agreement as equal partners in the work of the Kingdom of God. Indeed, without the valuable partnership with the gym and other partner organisations, the church would only have a miniscule mission, a very doubtful future and would be unable to develop or deliver a Kingdom of God theology and spirituality. And worse, the local neighbourhood people, the people associated with the organisations and the people receiving much needed services for the public good; would be denied their place in the family of God besides having no opportunity to play their part in it as well. The under-used, out of date, premises would offer no or very limited scope and the church people and congregation would retreat into a small enclave which, by its very un-diverse nature, would be seen to be and in practice would be exclusive.

There were varying degrees of participation in the work of the Kingdom of God by Brownley Green's partner organisations, but if this community fun day established anything theological and spiritual, it was the fact that this event was different from many others and that alone made it an extraordinary occasion. The feeding of the five thousand was unmistakeably extraordinary, and key to that success was its solidarity; being a brother, a sister, a mother to one another. Another key was a diverse community, sharing what each happened to have with one another and appreciating the real value of sincere relationships. And yet another was being open to new opportunities as and when they present themselves by doing things in faith and faithfully discharging them, before red tape inhibits and frustrates God-inspired enthusiasm and spontaneity.

Kingdom of God work, especially when it is the foundation of everything that is to follow, cannot be achieved without hard work and an absolute determination to succeed; there is no easy way. But there were significant occasions when, years later, it appears that a destiny has been achieved and the extraordinariness of the occasion is apparent. Much of Christ's teaching on this occasion at Brownley Green, was acknowledged, confirmed and made real in the behaviour and in the sheer life-style of the event itself. Out of a small dedicated mixed aged Sunday congregation has grown a much larger and impressive family of God, a diverse community of many parts but one wherein the Kingdom of God truly dwells.

His name is Bob and this man's relationship with Brownley Green is a reminder of the request sent to Jesus to heal a centurion's servant from his illness. The elders of the Jews delivering the request said of the centurion, "This man deserves to have you do this, because he loves our nation and has built our synagogue." Bob loves Brownley Green and has worked as a volunteer for the good of the church and people there. These are some of his comments that typify his commitment.

"The atmosphere, the spirit of the place is humbling. When I have been helping in the community bakery with fellow human beings, some with difficulties to overcome, they looked at us as strengths, as trust, as support. It's a lovely feeling to give so much back to them which made a big difference. They would tell you their stories and you realise what fantastic people they are and in comparison, appreciate how fortunate you are, they are, all of us are."

One day project manager Jason shouted over to me, that he had come, with a community of people, to make bread and us chuckling at the same time, "These lovely people also have special needs but they were going home with bricks!" Well, they were not actual bricks; they were the loaves of bread that hadn't risen sufficiently before they were baked!

Bob spoke of the poor resources available at the time of launching the café and about the huge respect he had for the individuals who grew in strength. He reflected upon the place of the gym in the overall scheme of things, its purpose and its work and the many times he was impressed by the clientele who used the gym; the aspiration of the gym's manager and the way he designed and got his websites up and running, indicating that everyone from whatever background or whatever limitations can aspire and build up self-esteem. And then, to quote Bob about someone who often spoke negatively by saying, "This will never work", Bob comments that every time the person he was speaking about, spoke in that way, what was sure not to work, did work!

The Community Shop operates from a portable cabin housed on the church grounds and as one of the regulars there, Bob was able to appreciate its purpose. "It drew people into the place and besides being a charity shop, the cabin was best suited as a meeting place, a communal place where all sorts of people's business and well-being could be aired, knowing the response would always be pastoral and always encouraging."

We do not know and cannot tell what on-going impact the occasion of the feeding of the five thousand had upon that vast crowd; what we learn and deduce from the event itself has to be sufficient. We can appreciate it as a one-off event in its own right and in that sense it fulfilled its purpose in the most dramatic and miraculous way imaginable. Similarly, open days, fun days, carnival days at Brownley Green come and go and each one creates its own character and setting, but on this particular occasion, likened as it was to the feeding of the five thousand, it can similarly be viewed as a one-off event sufficient for that 'moment-in-time'. What we do know is the way the event brought together the extremes of that diverse multi-purpose and many-peopled community and by so doing, revealed a family of God whose sharing and celebratory atmosphere had all the markings of the Kingdom of God. Such was this revelation that every person was able to be part of God's Kingdom not by consent, membership or by entrance fee, but by their own right and by their relationship with one another and everyone who was there.

SOUTHSIDE SPEECH & DRAMA STUDIO

The hall was crowded. All the seats were taken. The technical experts operating the lights and music were standing by. The three VIPs were shown to their seats at the front. Stage hands were at the ready and the fervent atmosphere was buzzing with excitement. The curtains opened and the show took off.

This was the annual performance by every one of the forty-two speech and drama student performers from Southside Speech and Drama Studio. They were performing Bugsy Malone and by the end of the last curtain call, you simply knew that everyone in the house had just experienced the most outstanding performance by anyone's standards. Sitting there quietly in the audience I knew something of what the occasion represented in relation to the children and young adults taking part and impressed, as I was, it was their demeanour collectively and individually that excited me most.

Southside Speech and Drama (SSD) was a partner organisation alongside the six others that made up Northenden Community Projects (NCP) based at Northenden Methodist Church. Meeting on Saturdays at the Day Centre used by the National Autistic Society, children and young adults were introduced to the performing arts and given expert tuition and individual life-enhancing guidance. The classes concentrated on improvisation and scripted work, poetry, prose and sight reading, all of which helped towards self-expression, confidence building and an increase in the students' own self-awareness.

Sitting as I did from time to time on the floor during their Saturday morning classes, leaning against the wall, I would silently watch them and was always aware of some of the young performer's vulnerability coming as they did from insecure and dysfunctional families. I could see the ones who were tentative, shy, nervous, often borne out of low self-esteem or anxiety, for such was their plight and their background. I recall conversations with their tutor and founder of the studio, "You can see, almost touch the positive changes that began a transforming process in one individual after another and change them into confident self-respecting persons in their own right." Not exactly the setting of the Last Supper, the Transfiguration or the Emmaus Road, and yet the similarity with confidence building and an assuredness beckoning the individual to some form of purposeful future, was striking. Noticeable also was the spiritual approach by the tutor to the student, with clear overtones of Christ's approach to the disciples and people he counselled. This was one of those occasions when recognition of the Kingdom of God is not confined to any one place or people, but recognisable in situations of trust, counsel, befriending, guidance, supervision and tutoring.

The excitement created at the annual performance was one of pride and achievement. Pride manifested in family and friends and achievement credited to the individual him/herself and if that is not excitement enough; there is a greater excitement of a human and spiritual quality. The human aspect is evidenced when emotions are stirred - and stirred they were by tutors and key eyewitnesses to the magnitude of the human endeavour involved and accomplished. The part that is manifested through achievement speaks volumes about the transforming process that will have played its part in the development of a person's distinctive character and the way that person's spiritual persona is expressed through their ever creative individuality.

Christ's references to the Kingdom of God and the way he associated those references through parable and every-day happenings can equally be associated to these individuals, coming as they do from a variety of backgrounds and situations; and that makes the connection between these performing youngsters and that same Kingdom vivid.

The children of the Speech and Drama group were brought to a place where the spiritual presence of Christ was not only expected to be present, but where it was discernible. Such was the empathy and sensitivity of the leaders to the children and young people and shown through their interaction. This brings into a contemporary setting the message of Christ to his disciples in Mark 10: 13-16 - "Let the children come to me, and do not hinder them, for the Kingdom of God belongs to such as these."

Another way of appreciating this is by relating the value to the speech and drama students of their classes and performances, to the values Christ gave to individuals in particular circumstances of his day. The end result is the same, in that their self-esteem, their confidence, their place in society and their integrity as a human person and their worth as an individual, is given due recognition in its own right. These are 'signs' of the kingdom Jesus frequently alluded to in his phrase: "For theirs is the kingdom of heaven." And in Matthew 5:3 "Blessed are the poor in spirit, for theirs is the kingdom of heaven."

It should not be surprising to discover in the spiritual overtones that accompanied answers to Southside Speech & Drama's questionnaire, an overriding philosophical approach by them that was very similar in essence and substance to a theological annunciation of God's Kingdom. Examples of this are noticeable and noteworthy in the following extracts from that questionnaire:

What are the spiritual values of your work/services?

We provide an environment for children to stretch themselves, make new friends and learn new skills because drama is about growing up in a world that is all around them, to the point where they belong and feel a responsibility to it. As leaders we keep giving and never stop giving to the children and young people whatever they need in order to learn more about themselves, more about each other and how to form relationships with their world and the world's people. And it is more usual than not, that they also give back to us at SSD a quality of relationship and personal maturity, that is beautiful and enriching, but the onus is on us to keep giving ourselves and never stop giving.

How do your clients/recipients benefit from your services?

All of the children and young people (students) irrespective of their background, circumstances and family history improve and develop their individual characters. They become more in touch with their whole selves and so begin to understand themselves better and know what makes them tick. This process is enhanced through the positive relationships they form with their contemporaries, appreciating and also benefitting from the diversity the different positive and negative family situations give them. The bonus for them is the achievement of real certificated examination results and that is something not on offer in state schools. The examination process is run independently from SSD and accredited by Ofqual with graded and diploma qualifications in drama and communication from the London College of Music Examinations Board. Qualifications are also supported by the University Quality Assurance System and now qualifications taken with us give points on the UCAS tariff for university entrance. All of this means the awards they receive and qualifications our students gain can be a real foundation for a future career in the arts.

How would you describe your relationship as a partner organisation alongside the other organisations?

It was good and it was mutually supportive. The Northenden Players not only offered the use of their lighting and sound equipment, but Nigel was always ready and willing to give a hand which was one reason why our annual performances were so technically brilliant. Similarly with CPM School of Dance and the times we needed to use the toilets or kitchen which meant walking through to the other end of their dance hall, the partner relationship was always noticeable in the welcome they gave us despite our intrusions. Communication via emails kept us in touch with each other and on the occasions we all did our 'party pieces' as we did I remember on one particular Open Day and for a church service on Remembrance Sunday, made you realise the positive-ness of relationships and their value.

How did you become involved with the Church or with Wythenshawe Oasis?

I initially contacted several churches because churches usually have space with spare capacity, but only Northenden Methodist Church engaged in conversation with me. The minister was very welcoming and I could see the church was in the throes of developing community links. We worked out a simple form of contract and SSD quickly got underway.

What do you think you originally 'signed up' to with the Church or W.O.?

It was most definitely a family because the church believed in what we were doing and in the social / educational nature of our work. The other aspect is support because the church through the lovely person who oversaw the letting arrangements promised to be supportive and she always was.

What do you think the churches & W.O. are about?

All about communities and linking organisations together as part of an over-arching community togetherness.

Can you describe your relationship as a partner organisation alongside the other organisations?

We were one among the others and respected them for what they were doing and achieving as much as we did for ourselves. When occasions arose to be supportive or take part in co-operative events, we did so like in the Remembrance Service simply by being there with the British Legion and others let alone our participation in the service itself.

Can you describe what the minister's role was and his professional relationship with you in relation to your organisation's work?

He was always a light at the end of the tunnel and his and our relationship was always on a professional basis.

Have you over the course of time heard the term: 'Kingdom of God'?

Yes the minister himself has used it.

Now here is a question to you, the reader of these tomes. Have you ever thought this way about the parable of the Prodigal Son sometimes called the Two Sons? Both sons needed showing to them the hidden potential that was deep inside them. The younger son discovered his potential the hard way, by leaving the family and going through a 'wilderness' experience, whilst the older son stayed behind and carried on doing what he always did and had no notion there was more to life than the usual daily routines. The younger son, may not have gone through a massive personality change, though that would have been noticeable in part, but he did go through a realisation experience and was able to appreciate potential within himself he hadn't seen or noticed before. In that sense he became a different person; he understood himself better, with a clearer understanding of his 'whole self'. With confidence back on track and low self-esteem banished. He was able to face a new future, a future of hopes and expectations and success. The older son showed potential through his loyalty to his work and through his consistent closeness to his father, but unlike his brother, who discovered his potential for himself, the older son needed his father to spell it out to him: "My son, you are always with me and everything I have is yours." In other words, the scene was set for the older son to develop further his skills and his knowledge in order that one day he would take over and keep the family business on track as an enterprising going concern.

Given their potential, we know not what either son might have made of himself, only that in telling the story, Jesus was hinting at the discovery of a God-given life of fullness, of high expectation and immense worth to themselves as individuals and of particular value to others. It is those same distinguishing qualities that characterise the work of SSD and draws out of the young people the potential that is inherent within them. They do not have to go through a 'wilderness' experience or have things spelt out to them, as the two sons did, but they clearly do discover their potential.

A number of lessons may be learned by the church in particular from SSD involvement and relationship with the church and with other partner organisations.

- There is an immense amount to be gained from watching an activity and listening and then comparing and contrasting the 'essence' of the performances with Christ's response and subsequent teaching to an individual's need for a higher purpose. Examples of Christ's teaching with that emphasis are many.

- There is Zacchaeus and the Demon-possessed man from the region of the Geresenes.

- Nicodemus who came to Jesus at night

- The story about the Pearl of Great Price and the parable of the Talents.

- The conversation with the woman at the well.

- The feeding of the Five Thousand and not least the contribution / participation at that event by the boy himself with the five loaves and two fishes.

Such an exercise can be a revelation in itself and enable the observer to appreciate subtle and profound ways the 'gospel' Jesus was proclaiming can be viewed in the spirit and in the human endeavour of these young people performers themselves.

- Give true acknowledgement to the guidance, counsel and the ways tutors and teachers alike are role models to their pupils. The sensitivity shown, the encouragement given and the genuine interest in their welfare and their individual futures are second to none. When those qualities connect with the skill that is used to develop the inherent and personal potential of each individual, a spiritual approach and relationship of considerable depth is very noticeable as are the positive and transforming outcomes evidenced in the individuals themselves. Similarly many an excellent preacher, Sunday School teacher, God-parent and church youth worker will have given this to their subjects, except in the SSD context it is often the case that a consistent holistic and comprehensive coverage of gospel values is given and received.

- When some of the young performers participated in the Remembrance Sunday service in church as members of one of the partner organisations, it was noticeable in the atmosphere created by some members of the regular congregation that such involvement was considered unusual and could have been a questionable assignment to undertake. But as co-members of the one Family of God and appreciating the true definition and understanding of what 'church' means and implies, does more than merely suggest members of SSD are as much part of the church as the individuals comprising the church congregation. Just as the 'church' is represented in its meetings and through its own organisations, so SSD is as much the authentic 'church' in their sessions on Saturday mornings. A misunderstanding of this concept can occur almost by default and demonstrates the need and value of mutual interest and support in one another's endeavours.

- To summarise: Just as the Kingdom of God was always weaving in and out of the work of SSD, so this thesis claims that SSD was as much the authentic church as other partner organisations and that includes its local Methodist Church hosts. Such a concept, indeed such an acknowledgement, can be a difficult hypothesis for some church people to accept or appreciate. When an organisation as that of SSD exercised such a partner relationship with the church as it did, lived out a philosophical dictum conversant with the work of the Kingdom of God and bore the hall-marks of that Kingdom; sitting on the floor and leaning against the wall observing the speech and drama studio in action as I did, the truth in the realisation that SSD are the 'ecclesia' (an assembly of the people of God for the purposes of God) in their way as the church congregation is in their way, made both the church represented through its congregation and Southside Speech and Drama through its members and work, co-equal in the one great universal family of God.

- Partnerships and relationships similar to that of South Side Speech and Drama's relationship to their host church can be ambiguous. Ambiguous primarily because of a lack of clarity as to where the organisation's relationship truly sits with 'The Body of Christ', the church as termed by the apostle Paul. That is by far the fundamental question and it is asked of all the partner organisations owing to their involvement and contribution to the work of the kingdom of God.

- A cursory glance at a definition of 'The Church' is as interesting as it is revealing as this excerpt from 'A Dictionary of Christian Theology' edited by Alan Richardson published by SCM Press asserts:

"The Church is a sign and organ of Christ's presence. Present-day ecclesiology involves a close study of the relationship of Church and ministry and of the Church to the Kingdom of God. This latter issue arises from the observation that the kingdom receives a primary emphasis in the preaching of Jesus but has little direct attention paid to it in the rest of the New Testament. The tendency in past ecclesiology has been to equate the kingdom of God on earth with the Church; the tendency today is to see the Church as the instrument of the kingdom. Yet another aspect of the doctrine of the Church is its relationship to the world, arising in part from the study of mission as a theological concept and the recognition of the need for the Church to be open to the world which is God's creation."

This not only endorses my claim that church and partner organisations alike have been working as equals in their work of the Kingdom, but the organisations can be viewed as an authentic instrument of the Church and a revelation of God's redeeming presence in the world. Such an acknowledgement is an innovative concept in itself, but its radical nature is perceived in the way it leads us to see partner organisations as well as churches, playing a crucial role in incarnational theology; by that I mean, their work and their presence is a manifestation of God in human form.

THE RUMMAGE

If the title of this particular project conveys the overtones of a glorified jumble sale or something resembling an in-house car boot sale, you will be hugely mistaken. Similarly, the biblical story of the Great Banquet in Luke 14 and the Feeding of the Five Thousand in the synoptic gospels and John, appear to be perfectly matched in identity and substance as examples of Kingdom values among a disparate and large community of people, corresponding to the hordes at the rummage sales. Yet despite all the similarity and connections with the rummages the two stories offer, it is the primary text of the story about the Sheep and the Goats in Matthew 25 that describes best its vital message and aligns it correctly with the core function of the Rummage Sales.

Every rummage and that means every month, the people of the local neighbourhood queue up in anticipation of a good worthwhile and profitable event. And as soon as they make their grand entrance the whole place comes alive as a community that keeps re-igniting itself. There are in fact two communities, one being the large number of volunteers who oversee the whole event and the other being the local people who are the patrons of it, yet they very quickly merge into just one big colony. Evidence of that is visible in the renewal of greetings and friendship that characterise the bonhomie and spirit of the whole place, as stories are relayed and volunteers up-dated on family news and personal concerns.

Initially the locals (patrons) make a beeline for the bargains, the essentials and the particulars, but when that frenzy is passed they soon enjoy the food and frolics the café offers and that is when the spirit of friendship, comradeship and care becomes most noticeable. But all of this is preceded with days and weeks of preparation. All the numerous items for sale at extremely low prices are collected from door to door over a wide geographical area and they include large pieces of furniture as well as everything you could imagine is needed to fully equip and furnish a home, including garden, kitchen and electrical accessories. It requires a huge commitment by the volunteers on the days of the sales themselves, but also in the painstaking care and detailed planning that makes sure everything is properly sorted and displayed.

All the rooms and every available space is used, such are the epic proportions of the events, the scale of the resources available and the masses of people, families and children that flood the place. In no time at all the throng of people and their clamour to be the first to pick over everything creates a buzz and huge family atmosphere that dominates the whole scene. It is obvious the place is not unfamiliar territory to them, particularly among those who are always coming and going to one activity or another throughout the week, but on rummage days especially, all the signs point to the place being their domain and they are at home.

From time to time the market place atmosphere lends itself to various promotions, be they in-house services like physiotherapy, chiropody and podiatry, or campaigns, welfare concerns and general publicity. And there are always some specific personnel mixing and milling with the crowds including myself as the local minister, in order to 'pass the time of day' or enter into conversations of a more personal / serious nature. Inter-relationships as these become important and invaluable for on-going pastoral care as many a hospital visit has resulted from such encounters and the 'family spirit' thus generated, becomes a true acknowledgement of (the family best described as) the family of God.

The title: 'family of God' in relation to the rummages is not used lightly and, as will be shown and explained from among the vast community of people, there are those who disclose a certain side to their characters that is very revealing. They are a diverse and miscellaneous community of people of all ages and backgrounds and fall unequivocally into that category associated with Christ's work and ministry; the 'humble and poor'. And with such a large body of local neighbourhood people so described, it is easy to appreciate the specialness and relationship-binding togetherness the rummage sales offer and accomplish.

As with society generally, there is always a minority of people at the rummages who are not necessarily the image of Christ in disguise, but more like cheats and thieves who do indeed try to be in disguise but only for their own profit. Barely a rummage goes by without something of value being stolen, stories that somehow don't ring true and some suspicious characters that enjoy bending the rules. They belong and play their part alongside everyone else and help to make it a diverse and universal community. You only have to look at some of the notorious characters Jesus encountered and some of the questionable places he visited, not to mention the ever critical Scribes and Pharisees, to appreciate the value the Kingdom of God is to all-embracing and inclusive communities. The rummage crowd is no exception.

In keeping with all the other projects and project work, the rummage sales are governed by a strict principle: to serve the people, especially those with the biggest needs, and accept everyone as a brother and a sister of the one community. That being the case, it is not surprising to discover in the midst of the rummages a real therapeutic community with some people, especially among the volunteers, going one extra mile after another, whilst others metaphorically speaking give also their shirt. Indeed, people's entire homes have been furnished including the laying of carpets with a minimum or nil cost to the home provider. This generosity is of particular significance because it is a generosity that is always available, always selfless and sacrificial in nature, always there as a way of life without pretension fuss or consideration. It is entirely un-knowing yet, its quintessential distinctiveness is in its innocent giving of itself without the expectancy of anything in return, any reward or acknowledgement. Such generosity is not the monopoly merely of one or two individuals; it is simply the true character of the rummage sales and the ethos that they generate which is noticeable in volunteer and patron alike. If a benefactor were asked, "Do you realise something? What you just did was at considerable cost to yourself and yet you did it just for me." It is highly likely that those who showed that sort of generosity would not have themselves appreciated that they were being generous. That is the fundamental nature of the generosity shown at the rummages by some volunteers in particular and some patrons too and it has huge consequences; it goes to the core, to the heart of Kingdom of God values themselves.

It is appropriate to pause at this point and remind ourselves what is meant by Kingdom of God principles and Kingdom values especially as they are much used and emphasised in these writings. A definitive description of Kingdom principles and values as they apply to this thesis are explained in the section 'Kingdom of God for Everyone', so it is sufficient here to give but a simple description.

Jesus lived out his beliefs through his own life-style and used them to govern his code of ethics and to secure a given standard of morality. Woven into this may have been rules and regulations he adopted as a means to be clear concerning the value and worth of the principles he chose to live by. Principles are fundamental norms and rules that represent what is desireable and make a positive contribution to an individual, a group of people or to an organisation. Values are derived from our principles and they determine our actions, what we do, how we behave and conduct our lives. They influence the way we make choices and how we are judged according to our actions. When principles and values as these are woven into the fabric of Christian spirituality, they become a most useful and important code of practice and that is crucial in relation to the running of the rummage sales. Earthed as they are in the principles and values of the Kingdom of God, the rummages in solidarity with all the other churches project work, remained true to these practices.

The generosity shown at the rummages are an expression of Kingdom values. It is enveloped in the word 'love' but not in the over-used and over-simplistic way it is commonly used. 'Love' as expressed in relation to the Kingdom of God has its own distinctive and profound meaning. It originates from the Greek work 'agape' meaning to love sacrificially, to give without expecting anything in return, or as Mother Teresa said, to love until it hurts. This takes us to the heart of the Matthew text which speaks specifically of 'agape' love in relation to generosity innocently shown to an individual and that individual as the recipient, becomes the person of Christ in disguise; Matthew 25:40 "Truly, I say to you, as you did it to one of the least of these my brethren, you did it to me."

This forms the central theme of the parable known as, 'the sheep and the goats'. It is couched in the setting of the last judgement and highlights two groups who come across people with different needs. One group ignores them and offers no help. The other group selflessly attends to the people's needs. The key message that underpins the parable is explored and explained a little further on. It is the people in need and unknown to both groups of people who become the person of Christ. The disguise is well concealed so much so that the group who showed no interest in the people with needs and wished when it was too late that they had known, were disappointed and were refused entry into the Kingdom, whereas the group who showed kindness in their responsive actions, were applauded and welcomed into the Kingdom. A 'them' and 'us' scenario as suggested at the conclusion of this parable, can infer entry into or participation in the Kingdom of God is not inclusive as this thesis claims. But it is the case that anyone from any background and circumstance can be the person characterised, in this instance, as a sheep. The important message being, the Kingdom of God is indeed accessible to any individual.

The Kingdom of which Jesus speaks is not a distant possibility, nor a figment of the imagination, but something that is in the here and now. It is the Kingdom of God. Where Christ-like love is, the Kingdom is. And if Christ is manifest in human beings - in individual people and, according to the story, encountered through the generosity of someone attending to their 'brothers/sisters' needs, as happens at the rummages, it is entirely appropriate to say of the rummages;

Christ is there, just as it is right and proper to say, the principles and values of the Kingdom of God are also there and form the bedrock of the events themselves.

Events like the rummage sales, which create their own ethos and acquire a distinctive culture, lend themselves to sayings like, 'you can put your finger on it', or 'you can feel it'. It is not the case that in those situations you can physically do those things, but you can nevertheless be convinced yourself about a particular truth, or a fact about which you whole-heartedly believe. Subject to appropriate examination and critique, the assertion is made that during the rummage sales especially; the Kingdom of God was there in the midst of everything going on and as such could be described as 'aura'. Such was the atmosphere and geniality of the place that it had a distinct spiritual quality and presence about it, and this was over and above the invaluable service the rummages were to the neighbourhood and local communities.

Given that experience and understanding, an exploration of the text already referred to in Matthew 25:40 merits examination. The paragraphs that precedes the 'Sheep and the Goats' opens with the words: "The Kingdom of Heaven can best be illustrated..." Jesus then goes on to tell two stories obviously aligned to an understanding of what he was meaning by 'Kingdom of Heaven' but does so in the setting of a final judgement. By creating that futuristic setting, Jesus is making a major statement and purposely turns it into a stark and serious message. The message concerns those who are the 'least of these my brethren' and Jesus describes them as being those who are hungry and thirsty, those who are strangers, those who have no clothing, those who are sick and those who are in prison. Such characters are clearly represented among the rummage, clientele including a broad spectrum of people who are frequently referred to as being the 'humble and poor'.

Jesus' revolutionary and controversial message gets to the heart of what it can and should mean for us today. The two key phrases that stand out are: "my brethren" and "to me". 'Brethren' can mean people like those at the rummages. Indeed there will be those who will actually be hungry, be thirsty, be strangers, have very few clothes, be sick and some will have been in prison. But the categories also imply to people who may carry the marks of those human situations in and through their own lives and lifestyles. And the title: 'to me ', implies to Christ himself.

David Hill in his book 'The Gospel of Matthew', together with Edward Schweizer and C.G. Montefiore offer these elucidations: The brethren are not only nor simply people in need, because Christ saw himself as one with all those who needed help and support, and saw in any down-and-out person someone who he regarded as a brother or sister. Even the word 'these' as used in 'these my brethren' has a special meaning in the way Jesus used it. Because of its Semitic overtones consisting of languages from Afro-Asiatic cultures, it refers to all people without exception. It tells us that Jesus was not referring just to his own disciples. He really did mean people who were literally hungry, thirsty, strangers, without clothes, sick and prisoners – (the humble and poor). It is generally agreed that as Christianity became known and grew, the value Jesus placed on the soul of a person gained momentum among the first Christians against the background of a Roman and heathen world. And such was its power of influence, that the teaching included every human soul and not least among them were the humble and poor. These were people who were always considered beyond the pale, but in Christian terms they were of equal worth to anyone else. This was like announcing the earth is round and not flat as everyone believed. No wonder Jesus and the first Christians were persecuted! Matthew 10:40 quotes Jesus: "He who receives you receives me, and he who receives me receives the one who sent me." This is a further claim by Jesus that an act of kindness done to an individual can mean that it is done to Christ himself.

It was before the days of risk assessments, being accompanied on visits by a second person and all other issues appertaining to safe guarding; as it was also before mental hospitals were withdrawn. Robert, whom I visited regularly, was sitting at the table eating his lunch and I was assisting him. Robert had been diagnosed with schizophrenia, endured a pink colour skin pigmentation over his neck and face and was not always rational.

On this occasion and having finished his meal, Robert asked me if I would go with him to his room. I knew this was a little out of the ordinary so I instinctively looked around this large common room to see if I could attract the attention of a member of staff, not a soul in sight. Walking slowly with Robert out of the room to the corridor, I was still keeping an eye out for a staff member or anyone that would witness me disappearing with Robert, but again there was not one single person anywhere. Eventually arriving at Robert's door, he indicated to me to go into the room first and I immediately noticed that the only chair was furthest from the door by the window on this second floor building. Should I need one, I thought to myself, my only escape route was obstructed by Robert himself who had chosen to sit on his bed; I was virtually trapped. As Robert was speaking in his slow meandering way, I was visualising him going into one of his fits with all the anger and super-human strength he sometimes exudes. My mind was racing as I knew I wouldn't be able to escape through the window or make a dive for the door, so I decided if necessary, I could run around him by jumping on and over the bed at least it might confuse him and that would be my best option.

As our conversation was coming to an end, Robert stood up, turned to face me and began taking steps towards me and as he did so he opened his big broad arms with the obvious intention of engulfing me. I had no choice except to allow his arms, his body in fact to overwhelm me with a hug that was as gentle and kind hearted as it could be. And whilst being held in that way, Robert simply repeated several times one simple sentence: "Thank you for being my friend."

As I left Robert in his room, I stood still and silent in the corridor for a few moments and remember being a little emotional as I said to myself more than once, 'why did I distrust him, why?'

We place all kinds of categories on people, all kinds of conditions and peculiarities, all kinds of reasons that make them different and at the same time fail to see their own uniqueness and it's worse when we disallow ourselves to discover the 'other' in them. "For as much as you did this to one of the least of these my brethren, you did it to me." (Matthew 25:40)

J. Neville Ward makes this point when he says: "There are people for whom the Kingdom has been prepared, as a piece of music is made for the people who will play it." And then goes on to say, "They are individuals who are merciful in their moral assessments, forgiving in their injuries and able to make positive use of suffering."

The statement by Christ that he can be embodied in another individual, could mean the same as saying 'Christ is Incarnated' in another individual and that being so, it establishes an affinity with Christ that takes incarnational theology to a new level of understanding and appreciation is grounded in the Kingdom of God. The teaching, ministry and life-style of Christ and its association with incarnational theology is unequivocal.

Mention has been made about the rummages fulfilling the role of a therapeutic community and such was the giving and receiving by individuals within that setting, that considerable human empathy, sensitivity and sincerity became most noticeable. The one-to-one conversations, the inter-personal relationships, the overall ethos of a mutually supportive community not only enabled, but positively encouraged the spirit and person of Christ to manifest itself. To explain it another way, within that therapeutic setting and it may only be on specific occasions, the depth of sincerity in the sharing of concern and 'agape' love, is reminiscent of the values at the core of Christ's own life and ministry and as such, reveals a 'Christ-like-ness' that becomes in essence and in spirit, the person of Christ himself.

Visualise the scene, volunteers tired out from collecting rummage articles and effects, sorting out rummage articles and effects, delivering articles and effects – always making contact and visiting people in their homes. A whole colony of people weaving in and out of each other, buying and selling, eating and drinking, speaking and listening, looking and seeing as well as sensing something different, something important, something human and if only they realised, something divine too. The rummage first and foremost is a place of encounter. The person of Christ is encountered, the Kingdom of God is encountered, the Incarnate God is encountered and the people are truly the family of God – the holy family of God.

Here are some testimonials from individual rummage volunteers and patrons:

Chris:

(Chris is one of the regulars to collect and deliver rummage paraphernalia besides always being on hand to help and get stuck in, in a variety of ways)

"I really believe in the Rummage. We take stuff other people don't want and we can fill people's homes of those who have nothing and at the same time, we make money. It serves all causes equally and we feel better in ourselves for doing it. We honestly get to know people really well, like a husband and wife who are doctors. I know that getting stuff from them helps our friendships to grow, but it breaks my heart when I wonder how the husband is going to cope with a growing dementia. He is someone with a workshop and makes beautiful objects. He makes me realise we're a family and they, with all the others, are part of that family and every day and every week; it makes a difference, a very big difference."

4 volunteers talking together:

"It is the high point to my main work, people accepting each other as they are, the good bits and the bad bits and that includes us and all the volunteers. We are one big team with individual talents and work together respecting each other's gifts. We've seen people grow up and that's been a privilege."

Kath:

(Kath is the e-bay pundit and spends hours and hours e-baying item after item with much success)

"The rummage is fantastic, one of the best community projects I've seen and the money helps keep the church in good repair, but the community aspect is more important than the money. I think the money the rummage makes should go towards enterprises that will keep developing the community there, because the church building enables all sorts of activities to keep going and is seen as the centre of community life. I first started going to the rummage as a customer and then when a 60's sideboard was sold at just £3, I thought that was too cheap and suggested it should go on e-bay. E-bay gives you a much wider audience and therefore a bigger market and more money. So I volunteered to sell items, especially the unsold ones, on e-bay and I love doing it especially when I see the real value of the articles and the success we have selling them. I like too the idea that the e-bay money helps towards maintenance costs."

Sue:

(Sue is the founder and leader of the Young at Heart Club. She organises the weekly programme, does a few other inter-connected activities and is one of many helpers on rummage days)

"The reason for starting the Young at Heart Club was for Marie and Harry. I went to Marie's house and I was gob-smacked because she wasn't able to get out and meet people. Harry's house is my base for all my gardening tools. Despite his acute physical disabilities, he still tries to do things, his example is my inspiration. The club is for people who can't get out or go anywhere. Now we are a little family who look out for each another. It's not the church that's given me this enterprising spirit, it's the people. Church is really behind the times. I see what people have got although they don't realise it themselves, they have lots to give and share. My group has risen from five to twenty-five, we're a big family now, and it gives freedom for them to be themselves. My job is to try and resource the people so they can be resources to one another and that takes the responsibility to care personally for individuals. I call it mutual confidence building."

Chris:

"Another high point of my work is collecting stuff for the rummages and when we're doing the round of deliveries afterwards, it's all in the interaction with the people in their homes and sparse homes many of them are too and that to me is spiritual. Like the huge amount of donations we get and collect month after month all kinds of stuff, especially furniture, that to me is very spiritual, but I couldn't be myself, the person I am in church services. I feel more at home when the church is empty and feel part of the church most when it's crowded out with people at the rummages."

Chris spells it out in her use of the word 'spiritual'. The entire rummage and the other projects have a spiritual quality and depth about them that takes you to the soul of the action, and in a lot of instances, to the souls of individuals. Simple definitions of 'spiritual' and 'soul' are helpful and the Oxford Dictionary describes 'spiritual' as relating to or affecting the human spirit or soul, as opposed to material or physical things and defines 'soul' as the spiritual or non-material part of a human being regarded as immortal. It is when comparisons are made in the use of spirit and soul by Christ that insights into their meaning are particularly revealing. In reference to a person's particular character, in other words the sort of person they are, Jesus said, 'blessed are the poor in spirit' (Matthew 5:3) and at the time of his dying he said to his Father in Heaven, 'into your hands I commit my spirit.' (Luke 23:46). Likewise concerning the soul there are these references: 'Do not be afraid of those who kill the body but cannot kill the soul' (Matthew 10:28). 'What can a man give in exchange for his soul?' (Matthew 16:26). 'Love the Lord your God with all your heart and with all your soul' (Matthew 22:37). Jesus clearly appreciated 'spirit' as the heart of an individual or as Paul Tillich, a religious philosopher, said: 'the ground of our being' meaning 'spirit' indicates the nature of someone, the sort of person they are. In relation to 'soul' and claiming it is something indestructible, Jesus is saying the soul is the essence of a person, the centre or core of their uniqueness. It is what defines their individuality and combines their human-ness with their spiritual-ness.

To return to the biblical passage: "Truly, I say to you, as you did it to one of the least of these my brethren, you did it to me." This lies at the heart of the rummages and touches on the spirituality of both the people involved and the events themselves.

Through insights gained into the spiritual side of people's lives and the spiritual-ness of places and occasions, plus a similar acknowledgement of a person in their soul-like-ness, the text quoted above goes to the heart of the matter and to the heart of this thesis. Relationships between many a rummage person is both human and spiritual and, in particular instances, is of a considerable depth, making the relationship as much with the person of Christ as it is with the individuals themselves. When the full significance of that is taken into account, it is possible to say that this is the method by which the risen Christ has returned and continues to return and dwell in and with humanity. It is a continuing process of the Incarnate God who identified himself with humanity in the person of Jesus and continues that identity through people who are themselves a revelation of Christ. Conventional teaching of the Church locates Christ's return in a futuristic Second Coming. It is more than sufficient for me to believe that the second Coming of Christ, so called, is not something destined to happen in a future event, but it is and has been happening all the time through the guise of those who, known or unknown to themselves, have been a revelation of the very spirit and essence of Christ himself. This was powerfully illustrated in an event concerning Sue, the founder of the Young at Heart club, when one of her members died.

Sue was distraught and inconsolable. First because she thought she could have prevented Audrey's death and consequently felt almost responsible for it. Secondly, she was enduring the loss of someone she had become close to and thirdly, the club was not going to be the same without Audrey. There was going to be a change – something idiosyncratically missing. Audrey was simply a club member, like the others and club members come and go but I do not doubt Sue would react similarly if another member of the club died in similar circumstances. Such is Sue's love for her people that it is more than empathy and more than a human closeness. It is at the depths of her being (her soul) that has embraced the soul of another. That is 'agape' love. That is the fusion of two people's spirituality and that takes us to the heart of Christ's injunction: "As you did it to one of the least of these my brethren, you did it to me." Christ's spirit and presence is as much in the person being served or being ministered unto, as much as he can be in the person offering the agape love. In these relationships Christ is a real presence and the Incarnation a living reality.

NEW HORIZONS

As well as having a project name to signify the areas of work and ministry all five churches and partner organisations are engaged upon, New Horizons project's statement based at St. Andrew's Church was thus:

"To provide a place with facilities to meet people's special needs, through art work and work among young people and through assisted housing for young adults, in an environment where social inclusiveness is shown through sensitivity and respect"

It was one of those occasions whereby the brain recalls an event in the form of a still photograph and this one is even better illustrated as one of those black and white prints with brown edging! It was the church's weekly fellowship meeting and we were in the room where they customarily held their meetings. It had now been taken over by a new organisation called Signpost which had very recently taken out a long-term leasing agreement with the church.

So the fellowship meetings moved to a small, dingy and dimly-lit space that many years before had been the sleeping quarters for a Wesley Deaconess. In contrast with the image of their previous room, a small group of people now sat around an old table on old wooden chairs trying to convince themselves the place wasn't cold and damp but it was really! The space they occupied was very small because there was scarcely any other room save for a sink and draining board and two other cupboard-size spaces that used to be the Deaconess's shower unit and broom cupboard. And just to immortalise the scene, the place was dimly lit by just one overhead light bulb shielded by its old canvassed lampshade. However, what the picture doesn't show is the people's sheer accepting manner of this cramped, old fashioned, cold-looking and out-dated accommodation, at the same time as saying to myself, 'they can't go on like that'! And that was precisely what I as their minister said to them after saying it first to myself. Things did indeed begin to change and not just the Deaconess old quarters of long ago, but changes to the whole church premises which were considerable to say the least.

The church was opened in 1960 and the premises consisted of: a large church worship area seating 200, a large hall with a decent sized stage, a medium size hall, kitchen, medium size common room, small office room, small store room, large vestry/office, gents and ladies toilets, large storage space behind the stage and a cellar. The Deaconess's flat comprised a very small living area, sleeping area and, as already mentioned, an even smaller area for shower unit, sink and broom cupboard. There was a caretaker's flat which had a reasonably sized kitchen, bathroom, living room and two bedrooms. Placed strategically and built in a central eye-catching part of the estate on the corner of a major road junction, the church was a building to impress, but the church's heyday when all its premises were being used was relatively short lived and by the time of the mid 1970's its' population and its organisations were diminishing. At the time of the big review of all five churches in 1998, most of the church premises were redundant, only one organisation remained, the average number in the middle-aged to elderly congregation was 25 and the whole building internally and externally was in a desperately poor state of repair. The church being in exactly the same situation as the other four churches, also decided to work towards a new future, different from the past and one in which its emphasis would include the provision of resources and special accommodation for people with disabilities, learning difficulties and impairments and that is precisely what happened with enormous success.

A meeting not unlike the character and setting surrounding the small group of Believers in the Book of Acts 2: 42-47 took place in a church member's modest living room and there and then began the plans for a new future. With very similar solidarity, altruism and piety demonstrated by the young Believers in Acts, these five church members, 'believers' themselves and inspired by the principles and values of the Kingdom of God as they understood them, may not have realised then just how ambitious and far reaching were the plans they were initiating. Having discussed and agreed the church's 'specialism' and without wasting a second, we started looking through the 'yellow pages' telephone book to contact agencies and organisations from the world of disabilities. Such contacts, which were many, sowed the seeds for a feasibility study from which emerged major alterations to the church premises, major external repairs, installation of specialist equipment, new partner organisations who became long-term lease holders and the raising of thousands of pounds.

One of the first organisations to become a partner with the church under the project name of New Horizons was The South Manchester Mental Health and Social Care Trust and after exciting discussions about their vision and the availability and conversion of church space and resources, the creation of a day centre specialising in the wide subject of 'art' was soon under way. The name chosen for their enterprise was 'Studio One' and the space they began occupying was what used to be the caretakers flat. The main purpose of Studio One was to improve and maintain mental wellbeing through creative art as part of a recovery approach, whilst taking a personal interest in each individual appreciating the community aspect of the group as a whole. Activities introduced included: painting and drawing as initial subjects and as the services expanded, digital photography, animation, textiles, sewing skills and gardening were also incorporated.

The practical ramifications were as industrious as they were imaginative and exciting. Initially, the spaces being used were simply the rooms once occupied as a residential two-bedroomed flat, but the first reconstruction was knocking down the wall between one of the bedrooms and the living room, the wall to the bathroom was next followed by the corridor wall. The small end bedroom became the office which doubled-up as a church vestry but only for a limited time as more office space was required as members of staff increased. This was an innovative and buoyant time for everyone associated with New Horizons including of course the Church and Studio One themselves, especially as more and more people were coming to the art-based activities and the spiritually infused holistic approach of the talented artistes set the scene for a truly therapeutic community.

It was during this time that the space that was once the Deaconess's flat also went through a restructuring transformation. Dividing walls were knocked down and a new church lounge with open-plan kitchen was in place and being used. At last, the fellowship group with other occupants including a PHAB (physical & able-bodied) Club had somewhere comfortable and pleasing to meet, but that was short lived! The manager of Studio One was desperate for yet more space, so he came up with an innovative and challenging idea. Create a lounge/leisure space using the back half of the church worship area and install a modern tea-bar alongside the top end of the outer wall. I could see the advantage of utilising such under-used space, but was really unsure about building a tea-bar or kitchenette. The general idea was welcomed by the church especially as the church worship area itself had already undergone a transformation with a newly designed 'communion' area at the front of the church, a new and ultra-efficient heating system, new lighting, new seating as well as a complete redecoration and this made the whole 'chamber' a very pleasing multi-purpose space. This would enable the occupants of the church lounge to re-locate to new surroundings at the back of the church and Studio One could take over the church lounge as a workshop for textiles, photography and sewing skills. After more fund raising to cover costs, the lounge/leisure area with modern tea-bar was proving its worth in blessings, as was the new Studio One facility; and these latest innovations were part and parcel of the ever extending vision of New Horizons.

This was New Horizons, but initiated first by St. Andrew's church people, investing in a big way in the imaginative concept of the Kingdom of God. A second partner organisation Signpost, was carrying out similar ingenious schemes of work to Studio One with the spaces they occupied consisting of the whole of one side of the church building including the large hall with stage, the smaller hall, kitchen, common room, office room, store room, storage space behind the stage and the cellar. And in time they re-designed and refurbished all their area and met the £60,000 costs themselves. Through programmes of care and support, advice and consultative services, Signpost is a 'hands-on' organisation that works primarily but not exclusively with 16 – 25 year olds, to help them maintain a home-life that is safe and secure with the means to support themselves, to live healthily and be free from harm. A huge city-like housing estate as Wythenshawe, with its very diverse and sometimes 'unstable' population, emphasises the importance and valued work of Signpost in meeting the needs of very vulnerable young people and some very insecure young adults. Add to this other voluntary organisations that are also New Horizons partners in their own right and the work of the Kingdom of God in the proliferation of its principles and values is immense. The partner organisations included:

- A tea dance
- A local community theatrical group
- A social & recreational club for people of mixed abilities
- A knit & natter group
- A church congregation of people mainly from Zimbabwe

- A church fellowship group
- An Irish dancing class
- A Pentecostal church congregation
- A martial arts organisation
- St. Andrew's Church Sunday services
- Studio One
- Signpost

The majority of these organisations fulfilled with distinction the vital part they played in extending the Kingdom of God to individuals many of whom testify to significant and positive changes in their lives and circumstances, citing particularly: a new found confidence, potential they didn't realise they had, gifts and skills that had remained untapped, a trust in people they had not had before, joy associated with the making of new friends, a new freedom, respect for themselves, and a re-discovery of faith in the world around them. Featured on pages 151 and 177 respectively are two stories 'A funeral at St. Andrew's' and 'The man whose life was turned around?' They illustrate this distinctive ethos that was so prevalent.

All the organisations became team players in running New Horizons and making sure it lived up to its name and lived out its creed, even to the point of sharing responsibility for the maintenance of the whole building and grounds. But it is the people themselves, the individuals – managers, employees, volunteers, church folk and the wide spectrum of people in their activity-based organisations and clubs and their acknowledgement of a positive difference in their lives which gives credence to the involvement of the values embedded in the integrity and morality of the Kingdom of God.

The search for a new future began simply and innocently by half a dozen Wythenshawe people meeting in someone's modest living room. Through faithfulness to their vision, it was not only their church that found a new future, but a whole new family of God discovered a new destiny.

In Conversation with Matthew

Matthew has been manager of Studio One from its inception and worked tirelessly in securing the vision he and his colleagues clearly saw and in the progressive sightings they observed as time went on. To the question how did it all get started, Matthew travelled back in thought and memory and said in a matter of fact way, how he went around knocking on church doors because he knew churches frequently had spare under-utilized space and that churches were good places to engage with local people and their immediate surroundings. It was after sharing with me something of the vision Studio One could aspire to, that turned what could have been a faint hope into something dynamic, purposeful and community led. "At that time," Matthew went on…"Signpost, the young people's organisation had already installed themselves in the church and were pioneering their own industrious work with young adults. I could see the enormous advantage of working alongside an organisation like Signpost and creating an environment and base from which we both could pioneer our community initiatives together. In fact it was no time at all before New Horizons was formed with not just two but about ten organisations. The mere fact of signing up to New Horizons as a team player gave Studio One the opportunity to be part of a much wider range of activities and initiatives which was great and, I think, gave all organisations more scope and a complementarity purpose, ultimately; a broader mission and more creative activities for use as a healing tool." The questions continued likewise…

What do you think Wythenshawe Oasis and the churches were about?

"A community doing community work and involving the wider community over and beyond which the church could do on their own. It was from 2003 that we became involved and very quickly seized the educational and regenerative initiative alongside mental health personnel, in order to break down stigma and barriers that are too prevalent in society."

What did New Horizons stand for?

"It was a conglomerate of organisations working in our own fields of work part in partnership with each other. We all had a shared responsibility, we shared resources, welcomed everybody and took an active interest in the building and everything the place stood for."

Can you describe the contribution you made towards the common goal of all the organisations?

"We have always been supportive especially to new organisations as and when they came along and more importantly, that they actually felt supported and part of an over-arching organisation."

It is noteworthy here to illustrate Matthew's keenness in the sharing of resources by mentioning Studio One's vast array of everything arty, crafty and textile-y, and the way they made those resources freely available for use by St. Andrew's Saturday Club.

How would you describe your relationship as a partner organisation alongside the other organisations?

"We consistently adhered to New Horizons mission statement in the collective approach we showed to project work as and when that was possible. Overall, as neighbours especially when particular issues arose."

How do your recipients benefit from your services?

"As individuals they benefit in different ways; they acquire new skills, become more socially adept, general improvements in their well-being, an appreciation of the strengths and friendships in being part of a community, by being challenged in a positive way which leads to positive action on their part."

What do your patrons understand about the wider involvement of Wythenshawe Oasis or that by any of the five churches?

"People who are most aware are those who become involved in the wider or extended activities, like the art group that meets at St. Andrew's House or the social group who use the back of the church."

Can you describe what the role was by Rev. David Bown in relation to your organisation and its work?

"He was an enabler, offered space, helped to piece together the greater programme of project work and gave consent to the alterations and refurbishment of the premises."

How would you describe your professional relationship with David Bown?

"He was a representative of the Trust (Wythenshawe Oasis and the church) and we worked together according to proper professional practice, but he didn't let official rules and regulations frustrate or prevent the transformation of the buildings and neither the activities and projects."

What would you say are the spiritual values of your work/services?

"A lot of it is to do with creativity, the ways people express themselves through the medium of creativity and through their own spirit which is no-less a creative bundle of energy. When that creative spark within them is challenged, that too produces a spirituality that is unique to the individual."

Have you heard the title: 'The Kingdom of God?' If so, when and in what capacity?

"No."

Has there been a religious input if any by David Bown, Wythenshawe Oasis or the Church and can you describe what it has been?

"There is a spiritual element in and around the place in Studio One; and the church conveys a particular atmosphere or 'spirit' in which to do stuff. In terms of something 'religious', no, I would say that has a low profile in comparison with a high spiritual profile."

What have been the positives in your working with Wythenshawe Oasis or the church?

"Having an organisation to work with that has always wanted to be engaged in work with people and has been open to ideas and very welcoming."

What has been negative in your working relationship with Wythenshawe Oasis and the church?

"None really well; very few anyway."

Is there still more that could be achieved?

"There always is it's the nature of the work here plus the new initiatives you can dream up in order to extend and expand the essence of what this work with people is all about. But you need your own organisation or its parent funding body to believe in it to the extent of providing the resources."

How would you describe the philosophical background to your work?

"We provide a range of creative art activities/courses in the promotion of good mental health and well-being through a programme of activities. We believe in people's creative potential and in the personal goals they set for themselves, because art has a positive impact on people, their health and in their inner self."

Is there anything you would like to say or add to the discussion/questionnaire?

"It's been great fun and let me tell you what one of our people here said to us when he arrived one morning:" "...I used to see only a grey day before coming to Studio One, now I see colours in the sky." "Don't you think that captures the essence of looking, engaging, lifting the head up and being drawn into life in a more universal way?" I agreed and could see in that very simple testimony, the fusion of philosophical and theological togetherness articulated through someone's human and spiritual experience.

ANECDOTES:

The day centre manager & car park supervisor

I visited a local day centre for people with varying physical disabilities as part of an on-going research into new features that needed to be incorporated into our church premises. We were converting a redundant office into a changing room and toilet with tracking as part of our New Horizons project at our St. Andrew's church. After inspecting the one at this particular day centre, I was at the door saying thank you and my goodbyes, when the manager looking me straight in the eye began saying affectionate things about me. Scoring direct hits into the shy side of me and blushing profusely, I tried to waive the innuendos to one side only to be met with a barrage of more amorous-like phrases. Finally escaping the ordeal I soon discovered I could not forever hide from this person's extrovert desires. A wedding was taking place at St. Andrew's for two members of the Saturday Club. Now you have to appreciate there is well oiled networking between members of clubs similar to the Saturday Club, and the day centres were no exception. Not surprisingly, there were hordes of people from clubs, day centres and organisations turning up for this exceptional wedding. And where there are people with physical disabilities, there are lots of specialised vehicles with access for wheelchairs. As people were crowding out the church's spacious entrance hall, the car park was log jammed with vehicles and wheelchairs. Like Corporal Jones in Dad's Army, the day centre manager with amorous intentions and with all her extrovert energy, announced she was in charge and would get everything sorted out. And so with arms gesticulating and her voice booming, she proceeded to do just that. On entering the entrance hall for the umpteenth time, she came straight over to me and said, "I'm wearing bright red because you know why and I will be sitting on the front row so you will see me all the time." There were more episodes but these two are sufficient to indicate the tremendous camaraderie between what became an ever widening network of people and organisations. And between them all manner of resources were shared. Help, advice and support, and the all-important common purpose between them all being lived out. The Kingdom of God had truly descended upon everyone and particularly at that wedding on that day at St. Andrew's.

The mum's partner who didn't like my visits

I knew this girl from the days she and her brother were my house communion assistants, but many years had come and gone and the young communion assistant was now a mother of three lovely children. Having been badly treated by her first husband, she was now with her second partner and her oldest child had now reached secondary school age. I still kept in touch with the young mum but only visited the family home occasionally, but every time I did something was very noticeable. Her partner would never look at me or speak to me, not even a 'hello'. Either he would go into a corner of the room or as on this occasion, disappear into the kitchen. On leaving the house, I popped my head into the kitchen to be met by a very fierce caged dog while her partner and the dog's owner, did nothing to quell the animal, kept his back to me and didn't move or say a word.

How to be the strongest man

The strongest man competition was held on Brownley Green's Community Day featured above in chapter 4. Organised by the muscle-bound men from the church's gym, it was the annual event to discover the strongest man. A suitcase of heavy materials (probably bricks) had to be held waist high without friction for as long as possible. The man holding the case in that motionless state, the longest; would be the strongest man. Thinking the men from the gym were going to have a laugh, the cry went out, "Get the vicar and make him do it." Being the 'vicar' I duly complied despite being in a totally different league to the array of Mr. Universe muscles that surrounded me. The laughter however soon changed to astonishment when I won and accepted the coveted title of the strongest man, but that was not until the muscle men spent the rest of the day doing their level best to "beat the vicar." My technique? Simple really; holding the heavy suitcase waist-high in front of me, I simply kept counting in my head one to ten and every time I was nearing ten, I made myself believe I would start the next round of one to ten and I continued doing that until finally the strength in my arms had had enough. No-one messed with the 'vicar' after that!

CHAPTER 5

THE KINGDOM OF GOD SEEN THROUGH CONVIVIALITY AND THERAPY

T his chapter goes to the heart of being therapeutic communities, addressing needs and utilizing resources that will permeate people's circumstances in a spirit of friendship and trust.

"Put it here where you can see him."

CHILDREN & THE KINGDOM OF GOD

[Rules and regulations appertaining to safe guarding had not been established when the story in this opening paragraph took place. All safe guarding procedures in the subsequent stories were adhered to as a matter of course]

"Is David coming out to play?" If he was home with time to spare, yes he would join them for a game of football or something and occasionally three or four of the youngsters would jump into his car and drive the one and a half miles from the Frankley estate where they lived to the Waseley Hills, not far from what was the old Austin car plant in Birmingham. One particular morning all four of them were running down the side of the hill, with arms outstretched like aeroplane wings in full flight and each one as raucous as fighter planes. The person they would call to see if he was coming out to play was the local minister, who was also their neighbour and enjoyed the recreational times as much as the youngsters. With so much youthful energy and a real keenness to share it, the local minister gained a reasonable knowledge of the youngsters' family background and prevailing circumstances. Not unlike many children on the housing estate, the four of them had recently moved from the inner city to this new estate that bordered south Birmingham with north Worcestershire and where now these new roads and houses had taken over what was once lush farm land. This country scene, outdoor hilly environment and carefree atmosphere just over the way, was something very new to the families compared with the neighbourhoods from which they had come. Whether any of the young adventurers were experiencing difficulties or abuse like too many children were prone to was not known. What was known was the thrill and sheer delight they were getting from those outdoor pursuits. The question is: how can such simple outdoor activities with a few youngsters be described and interpreted theologically and spiritually?

Here are seven distinguishing features all of which played an important role in the creation of the open space games the youngsters found so enjoyable:

- **Trust**. They placed their trust in the adult that they would be safe with him, enjoy themselves and would be returned to their homes safe and sound.

- **Freedom**. They took full advantage of the freedom the open spaces gave them.

- **Recreation**. They relished their games and their whole bodies exploded in physical activity.

- **Imagination**. They indulged in inventive creativity and transposed themselves into all manner of characters and aeroplanes.

- **Individualism**. They found the solace and the space to be truly them-selves, without adult spying eyes or interference.

- **Solidarity**. They played and interacted together using social skills commonly associated with collective responsibility and that was revealed through the way they cared about each other and shared the games they played.

- **Nature**. They enjoyed to the full the natural environment, its invigorating spirit and weather-bringing elements.

The trust between the youngsters and the adult needed to be absolute without the smallest hint of doubt and that could only have been possible with unequivocal integrity in the adult.

The freedom of the open spaces gave the youngsters the opportunity to think for themselves, choose from their own set of choices and make their own decisions. That was how they were truly themselves.

Their recreation was the medium by which their physical creativity was woven into the tapestry of the natural environment of God's creation.

Their minds were open to explore and invent at will and see the world they were occupying at that time in their own unique way.

Their uniqueness through their own distinctive natures, characters and personalities was able to flourish and reinforce their individual identity.

Their togetherness was an important statement about their relationships; which were essential ingredients towards trusting and understanding one another and thus sowing the seeds of a mutually supportive community.

It was the physical environment that made everything they experienced and enjoyed. It enabled all their senses to come alive and to appreciate a world which was not small and compartmentalised, but open to unlimited possibilities.

In this next story two siblings of primary school age were waiting as arranged outside the gates of one of the churches for a lift to a children's holiday club where a week-long programme of activities was taking place. It was a drab, wet and coldish morning and the sight of the two children in their dirty flimsy clothes only reinforced the inclement conditions. Despite being rushed, I and my colleague made it on time but were immediately saddened and concerned when the children, in answering my question, said they had been there at the church gates for a considerable time. No wonder their flimsy clothes were pretty sodden and their hair soaking wet, but it was their overall unwashed appearance and unpleasant body odour that was most noticeable, very noticeable indeed. Delivering them to the activity-packed church, which had become similar to a children's centre for the week, they were received by friendly and caring supervisors, I made several mental observations as I thought about the two children and their circumstances. It was known that the two of them were very vulnerable to ill-treatment and even abuse. Home-life was grim to say the least and parental reputation left a lot to be desired as these two children were clearly undernourished and under cared-for. In fact I remember thinking, it was from the moment they came with us in the car that they were safe and able to have a sense of security and well-being, something that was clearly absent in their home-life and when they were alone on the streets.

The priority therefore was to get them to a place where they could thoroughly enjoy themselves, be properly cared for and be able to flourish in their own natural creativity. Each of the 'seven distinguishing features' mentioned above, suddenly became visible when these two sisters discovered the delights of the activity-packed children's centre - in a similar way to the four youngsters enjoying their outdoor experience on the Waseley Hills.

Children's work involving all organisations throughout the five church premises was considerable and they included the following:

- The 100 plus street-dancers at the Brownley Green church.
- The after school clubs at Baguley Hall and Lawton Moor churches.
- The speech & drama group and The School of Dance at Northenden church.
- The Irish dancers at Baguley Hall, St. Andrew's and Brownley Green churches.
- The junior club at Lawton Moor church.
- The Sunday Schools and the more recent Messy Church at Northenden church.

All these organisations with their highly professional and spirit-filled programmes of activities plus on-going pastoral care fulfilled, in every way, the same 'seven distinguishing features' being the hall-mark of children's work and care throughout the Wythenshawe Churches; such was the pioneering children's project work with partner organisations.

Vibrant and of the utmost importance as the children's work was, there were sad and difficult times as well. This sad occurrence concerned a pupil from the primary school, next door to the church, who attended the church's junior club. Naturally the club leaders were well known to the child and were more than mere leaders to her as they had a pastoral concern for the whole family and in that sense they were like guardians to all this family's children. There was one particular occasion when the child's distress became inconsolable, resulting in her running out of her primary school and making a beeline for her club leader.

This young person's home-life was a chaotic state of affairs with one parent an alcoholic and the other one too frequently in and out of prison due to drugs. She had many siblings and all of them were continually loved and cared for by the church, mainly through the superb pastoral care of the husband and wife club leaders. Many a time the children had breakfast with them and they were continually kitting the children out with new clothes but by the next week they would be back in their old ones, in the knowledge the new ones would have been sold. It took all the consoling powers of the family support worker from the school to coax and persuade the girl to leave her 'guardian parents' and return to school.

Such was the children's work and such was the immense compassion and personal involvement required by those who worked with the children, to the extent that they became essential role-models. It is, as already mentioned, a reminder of the true meaning behind the word 'love' so frequently used by Christ and quoted by New Testament authors especially the gospel writers. In its original Greek, it is 'agape' and means 'sacrificial love', the highest quality love that never tires and never expects anything in return. The reason why the junior club was so successful and always had a waiting list was because of the agape love which ran through everything the club stood for. The club was like a huge fisherman's net drawing in children from all manner of backgrounds and circumstances giving them a feast of activities and care. When appreciation is given to the values and principles attributed to the work of the Kingdom of God, and when children's work comes within that category, it is reasonable and admissible to link children's joy and fulfilment they experience, with actual blessing that is of God. And the same 'seven distinguishing features' mentioned in connection with the children who enjoyed the fun and frolics of the open space, were clearly visible in all the children from the many clubs and activities listed.

Over a period of years and with full parental permission, I had the pleasure of taking a friend's child plus grandchildren in my car to their primary schools and home again afterwards, but before returning home they always choose what they wanted to do with the hour or so before arriving home and that 'spare time' would nearly always be used imaginatively and creatively. And trip after trip to and from school I was awash with these children's wonderful imaginative stories which I'm sure were as real to them as the adult mind is to a good novel. Not unlike other children of similar age, their receptivity, their 'capturing the moment', the way their stories reveal a profound truth too often by-passed by the adult mind and delivered with the simplicity that gives its message a maturity unsurpassable, can be amazing. Such is the intellect and innocence of a child's way of looking at life and seeing themselves fully involved in it.

It is not surprising therefore when referring to the essential ingredients that characterise the Kingdom of God that Jesus should do so by placing children for-square at the heart of that Kingdom. "Let the children come to me, and do not hinder them, for the Kingdom of God belongs to such as these. I tell you the truth, anyone who will not receive the kingdom of God like a little child will never enter it." (Luke 18:16-17) If anyone can get a glimpse of the Kingdom of God Jesus is picturing or can catch sight of the Kingdom as something that is alive and not dormant, something real and not a fantasy, that is exciting and not boring, it is surely a child. And if that Kingdom, as articulated by Jesus, is such that it can be detectable through a child's imagination, creativity and innocence, Christ must also be inferring that the adult should see and accept that same Kingdom also in a simplistic way, but then encourage the intellect to see and accept its profundity.

It is helpful to be reminded of the seven distinguishing features that are a natural part of a child's character, they are:

A child's natural tendency is to:

- Have a trusting nature.
- Relish a real sense of freedom.
- Enjoy recreational activities.
- Use the power of imagination in authentic and creative ways.
- Be truly the individual they are.
- Discover a common bond with other children as a symbol of solidarity.
- Feel at one with nature and the world around them.

In contrast to the teaching element illustrated by Jesus in referring to a child's character in the text just quoted, an additional point which is the substantive one Jesus is at pains to enunciate, is all to do with the adult's approach to an understanding of the Kingdom of God. Unlike the average child, an adult will clutter his mind and his thinking with all manner of connotations that prevents him from seeing or appreciating, sometimes a simple truth Jesus is pinpointing. By citing a child's virtues, Jesus is trying to unclutter the adult mind and enable the adult to perceive the Kingdom from the viewpoint of a new mind-set, whilst taking nothing away from what should ideally, be the expected and accepted norms of an adult's approach towards children.

Right out of the blue one day a 9 year old boy with his two sisters who were 14 and 11, came and lived with me without any preparation or foreknowledge of it. It was while their mother was in hospital and their father under no circumstances was to know where they were or have any contact with them; and that was conveyed unequivocally to me. Despite their desperate circumstances, they quickly homed into an easy and relaxed family environment and the interaction between us all was exemplary. Being aware of their sad situation, I was deeply moved one day by something the 9-year old boy suggested accompanied with befitting gesture. He went over to the end corner of the window in my work room, picked up a very small framed picture of my father that was there and having asked who it was; he then placed it on the table next to my laptop saying: "You should put it here where you can see him." Suddenly I saw in this boy who is no different from most mischievous boys with the exception of his tragic parental circumstances; a sensitivity, tenderness and genuineness that spoke volumes about his true character in other words, his spirituality.

To me, it is that same spiritual quality Jesus emphasised when describing the kingdom of God as being like a child. But we have to appreciate the essential pith Jesus is highlighting; and that is a calibre of spirituality which transcends the quagmire of a child's messed up personal life. And that gesture from the young lad is the clue, his innocence enveloped in discerning sensitivity, takes us to the heart of the matter.

And that heart of the matter is reinforced by former director of Christian Aid Charles Elliott when commenting on the Beatitudes, especially in reference to 'seeing God' which he claims happens in the context of the Kingdom of God. I quote; "To promise to anyone that they would see God was blasphemous. To offer the Kingdom of Heaven or sonship of God to the poor and the persecuted was almost worse. These were honours that even the great patriarchs would hardly aspire to; and here was this brash young man (Jesus) scattering them around like confetti to the riff-raff. And he ends with this assertion, "There is nothing so threatening as a radical challenge to our secure values." But I would put it another way; there is nothing as enlightening as an instinctive gesture from a child that challenges our preconceived ideas and shows us a profound truth.

The approach Jesus is commending as entry into the Kingdom of God, ideally should be the same as an adult's approach towards children namely: to be honest, to be trusting, to be responsible, to be engaging and to be free of ulterior motives. With that level of integrity and uncluttered insight, there is every chance that the adult will 'capture the moment' and apprehend the unassailable truth about the Kingdom of God. Jesus presents it in such a simplistic way, almost too simplistically, but persuaded in that manner, the profundity of its truth can be realised.

The main thrust and motivation of citing so many different illustrations of pioneering project work by church and partner organisations in diverse contemporary settings, is to realise this fundamental truth: The Kingdom of God is the primary source of God's presence in both human and spiritual relationships. Its manifestation cannot be limited any more than it cannot know any end; but it finds its rightful place in all manner of circumstances and situations and among them not least, in the work and endeavours of the Wythenshawe churches and their partner organisations.

NEW DAWN CAFÉ, THE SATURDAY CLUB, MO'S SHOP

"Ask and it will be given to you; seek and you will find; knock and the door will be opened to you. For everyone who asks receives; he who seeks finds; and to him who knocks, the door will be opened." This text is from Matthew 7: 7-8 and brings together three projects and shows a commonality of purpose as well as giving expression to the text's original inference and a contemporary message.

There is someone in one of the five churches who never ceases to express his overwhelming gratitude for the kindness and consideration that is always shown to him. He often reminds his church people just how unsuccessful his search for a church that would truly welcome and accept him was and that is usually followed by expressing his joy and relief in finding such a community. Several years on and it has been to the church's fortuitous gain that he found his rightful place among them with no looking back.

It would be disrespectful to speak of this man's misfortunes except to say he is retired, lives on his own, has medical needs as well as other needs and spends a lot of time on his own. It is clear that his many needs, some of which can be considered acute, could be drastically eased and reduced by help from one or two members of the church congregation and without complication or stress, but nothing of course can be done without his personal consent and such consent is simply not forthcoming. Difficult though it may be and uncomfortably so, but it means the church community just has to accept this person's wishes and respect him for it. Not easy because his needs are acute and everyone truly believes the benefits he would receive would change for the better so much that affects his every-day life, but it is not to be.

Sometimes church communities have to understand and accept a person's appreciation of God's Kingdom even when it appears that that Kingdom is being enjoyed in short measure and they want above everything else for the said person to have it in full measure. It is obvious too through this person's endless gratitude, that the love and kindness he receives and the important sense of belonging he feels is sufficient, and that is a lesson we have to learn. For him, his experience of the Kingdom of God is complete and requires no topping up. It is as if he is saying, 'I have asked and it has been given me, I have sought and found it, I have knocked and have entered in'. It is in that spirit that three projects from different churches fulfil their individual enterprises and in their own way give an expression to the Kingdom of God.

1. New Dawn Café

One of the enterprises is New Dawn Café. It is open for business one day a week, offers simple and wholesome meals at extremely affordable prices and has a regular clientele with an atmosphere that welcomes anyone and everyone. There are highlights throughout the year which are reminders of the specialness of the café's community and the sensitivity that is shown towards one another. There was an occasion when one of the regular patrons was distressed and most upset. Sitting at her usual table and sharing the meal with those who knew her, she was comforted and not alone any more in her deep sorrow. She explained that her friend had died following an accident with one of

139

the city's trams and her sudden and unexpected death was too much of a shock for her. Before the end of the meal everyone in the café including the staff shared a minute's silence with appropriate prayers and the sympathy shown towards their distressed companion continued through personal contact on a daily basis.

As though by chance, or rather by a true sense of community spirit, a large proportion of the café clientele were in attendance at this person's friend's funeral who was herself known to many because she also sometimes came to the café. What was discernible at the funeral was the high level of support towards their distressed friend which was interpreted as a 'oneness' in spirit and in love. This was one of those occasions when café personnel, unprompted, gathered together, not to share a meal in the old familiar setting, but to share something far more human and spiritual which the café through its community setting had given them. Maybe on that occasion and in a slightly different way to the person highlighted in the previous story, the said café companion might have been heard to say, 'I didn't ask but it was given me, I didn't seek it but it found me, I didn't knock but the door was opened for me'. That best describes the place of the café in New Dawn's project work, in the neighbourhood from which the café draws its patrons and in the hard working volunteers who labour tirelessly week after week after week.

2. **The Saturday Club**

The Saturday Club is best described as a monthly get-together of people from a wide variety of backgrounds and circumstances, from people with learning difficulties and physical impairments, to those with mental issues and others with social welfare concerns and included the carers and helpers who are just as much part of the club as anyone else. In other words, the club is a community that is thoroughly inclusive and requires personal understanding and sensitivity by everyone to everyone. Meeting as it does at St. Andrew's in the church's project name New Horizons, the Saturday Club has use of Studio One's art and craft facilities as part of its recreational programme of activities. Besides socialising within its mix of games, meals, personal care and entertainment, the club organises outings and visits to places of interest; two such favourites being a community farm and the local fire station (especially the firemen in their uniforms of course!) But there was one particular occasion when everyone was able to make bread.

A ring of tables was positioned in the middle of the church sufficient for fifteen people to occupy table space to make their bread. Inside the ring of tables was the supervising baker who had already placed the separate ingredients, mixing bowls, jugs, chopping boards doubling up as surface mats plus some miscellaneous equipment for each of the club's new 'bakers'. Everyone made their dough in unison and eventually through the mixing of the ingredients, the kneading, moulding, proving and finally, the bread was baked to perfection and the 'bakers' were very happy and proud craftsmen and women. Each of the bakers took their specimens home and a true sense of achievement was as apparent as the crusty loaves were themselves icons to behold.

The sight of the loaves of bread symbolised a real sense of equality, an equality that gave everyone - club members, volunteer helpers, carers not only a sense of worth, but a value each other shared in equal measure and a common purpose that went beyond bread making, to the actual nourishment the bread would give family members gathered round the tea-table that evening. All are equal in the Kingdom of God, sometimes without asking, without seeking, without knocking. Like making a loaf of bread and everyone simply enjoying it together.

3. Mo's Shop

The sign on the port-a-cabin says 'Mo's Community Shop' but you have to go inside to find out what sort of shop! Lots of good clothing, some nick-knacks, white elephant merchandise, sometimes furniture and jewellery and then there is the tea & toast but over and above all of that is the chat, the conversations and if you were a fly on the wall, you would know something of the value of those discussions. Open two days a week as 'the cabin' to the locals, the shop is a hive of activity and a good place to get arms full of clothes. Clothes for sale used to be supplied by organisations with unwanted or out of date catalogue apparel. When that source dried up a couple of church charity shops in particular stepped in and made sure supplies would keep rolling in.

Getting back to being the fly on the wall, there was one particular day when the 'chat' was rife like a flock of gaggling geese that wouldn't stand still let alone quieten themselves down. The agitation which was very close to anger pitch was over someone who was in effect being 'evicted' from their house; not because they had done anything wrong or they were in trouble with the housing association, but because their neighbour had made life intolerable for them. The crunch came when evidence was found of a homemade fire bomb and the only way it seemed the situation could be resolved was by agreeing to move away to another house in a different part of Wythenshawe, and that felt to the family the same as being evicted. Well, this whole scene was being played out one morning in the shop and feelings generated were at fever pitch. I remember thinking to myself, week by week and month by month the shop here serves those who too often can feel the world passes them by or wonder just how they're going to cope. From the vantage point of 'the cabin', righting the wrongs in the world and protesting vigorously against the sort of injustice that hits the vulnerable more than anyone else is what they are about. I recalled the issue was in fact raised first in church on Sunday, but His sense of injustice and outrage only began to materialise among the shoppers in 'the cabin' and quickly began fuelling the thirst for right to prevail. It was at that moment I felt intensely proud - proud of the gang in the shop who were the beatitude people that day. Proud of the shop for all that it stood for and for being what the church isn't on Sunday's by actually making a stand in practical ways. Proud to liken them to the biblical prophets of the Old Testament and in the way they flexed their muscles in allegiance with the Kingdom of God. All are equal in the Kingdom of God and sometimes it is given without asking, found without seeking it, opened to you without knocking. This is because there are times when the church community needs also to do the answering as well as the asking, protesting as well as seeking and petitioning as well as knocking.

The text quoted from Matthew 7: 7-8 is often misunderstood and worse it is very commonly misinterpreted. It is over-simplistic to read it as though through prayer God will give us what we ask, enable us to find what we most want and open the doors to a future of our dreams. That does not speak of unselfishness as advocated by Jesus, it suggests the reverse. When the text is read in the context of the Kingdom of God, in your asking, the Kingdom of God will be offered. In the search for justice amid injustice, it will be found. In knocking at the door of the Kingdom it will be opened and to all who are sheltering and supporting.

The rehoused family settled quickly into their new surroundings despite losing a 3 bedroomed house for a two bedroomed one. But it meant they were free from the violent nature and hostile environment of their previous neighbours and that meant everything to them.

In their different ways and through their different settings the New Dawn Café, the Saturday Club and Mo's Community Shop play their part being the Kingdom of God for everyone and everything they stand for; compassion at a time of tragedy, equality in tasks of togetherness and justice at the expense of someone's adversity.

THE ART PAD

There are three characteristics that characterise the Art Pad. The group is a self-made small community of people. They all have a shared interest and possess a common flair and creativity. They manifest a collective responsibility and jurisdiction.

1. **A self-made community**
   Asked how they came together and one answer they gave was that they all graduated from Studio One at the same time and wanted to continue on a regular basis in one form or another. So they organised themselves into a group, took responsibility of the group, negotiated accommodation at St. Andrew's House and began meeting every week under the name of the Art Pad.

2. A shared interest

It would be easy to say their shared interest was simply in oils, water colours and drawing and it was, but what also clearly manifested itself was the interest they showed towards one another that was over and above their art work. The encouragement they were always giving to and receiving from each other; and the times they gave individual and personal support and counsel was second to none.

3. A collective responsibility

Their collective responsibility came to the fore whenever decisions were required and in the running or managing of the Art Pad but there was more. It revealed itself in the sense of 'ownership' not just of their group but of the venue - of St. Andrew's House itself especially during the times they were occupying the place. They had and showed responsible oversight of the building, one; through enhancing the character of the house by decorating the walls with their own pictures, two; by doing small maintenance work and showing respect to all users of the place, three; giving hospitality and acting as host to callers as this occasion illustrates:

The house kept a food store similar to a small food bank and welcomed callers requiring food. Someone called while the artists were in residence and in their usual hospitable way, one of the group members gave assistance to the caller and made sure she received her provisions. The co-operative nature of the service and its communal spirit was further illustrated when the same caller returned some days following and offered to sort out the food store and categorise the tins and packets of food in an orderly way as a favour for receiving the food. With the encouragement of art pad people, the caller did indeed sort out the provisions and refused the offer of more food because she said she still had sufficient from the previous time. It may be a small detail, but even this reciprocated personal interaction between the two occupants, showed evidence of a shared ownership. Just as the Art Pad didn't actually own St. Andrew's House as a legal entitlement, so neither did the caller own the provisions of the food store, yet they both felt at liberty to take the initiative over the period of time they felt part of the place, and that sense of incorporation was as important as it was real.

This poses the question: To what extent might the prevailing ethos and 'spirit' of St. Andrew's House on those occasions have created an atmosphere or related a sense of conviviality in the backdrop of shared ownership? It goes without saying that the sense of conviviality and collective accountability was also due to the fact that the Art Pad clearly fulfilled the brief of a therapeutic community, indeed that was the 'soul' of the community's togetherness. This takes us directly to the teaching ministry of Jesus and the way he propounded the view that the Kingdom of God was as much about society taking ownership of its responsibilities towards one another, as it was about individual recognition and acceptance of the values the Kingdom of God bestows.

ST. ANDREW'S HOUSE

The Art Pad serves as a good lead-in to finding out more about St. Andrew's House. It is the administrative home for Wythenshawe Methodist Churches and Wythenshawe Oasis and home to various organisations, community groups, meetings, parties and a food store. As a community house it offers space and facilities for in-house activities including office space and rooms for one-to-one conversations. It has good kitchen facilities and the walled grassed garden is ideal for barbecues. It is a resource and can be a haven, a meeting-point, an abode, a place to pop into for a chat and while you're there, the place gives the feeling it is yours and that just about sums up the place. Speaking of the garden and included in that are the surroundings, and it is more than appropriate to mention the person who single-handedly oversees that work. Gardener and maintenance man is Malcolm who does not just ensure everything is as it should be, but devotedly spares no effort making sure the whole place is always in pristine condition for its varied and many uses.

St. Andrew's House became a Community House whilst at the same time being the office base for the five Wythenshawe Churches and the registered office for Wythenshawe Oasis. In the past the house was the home for the Methodist minister and family. With no minister or other residents to house any more, and before its designation as a community house, discussions about its future included, among a variety of options, the possibility of returning the property to Manchester City Council. It would raise a financial reward as would letting the property which would give the advantage of securing a regular income. Priority in the decision making process was first and foremost; how could the house best serve the purpose the churches had committed themselves to, namely, to engage as purposefully as possible in the work of the Kingdom of God?

Consequently, the chosen option for the house was to be a meeting place and rendezvous for the local people and local organisations and to be the main base for administration; for the minister and the administrative assistant, for the work of the five churches generally and for the work of the churches' own charity: Wythenshawe Oasis.

The house did indeed live up to its stated aims and not only accommodated a variety of groups and organisations with office and space and rooms for individuals, but always sought to impress upon its inhabitants that they in effect 'owned' the space they occupied. This was important because if the house was to play its part in the work of the Kingdom of God, there would need to be a 'collective responsibility' by all inhabitants over the use of the house, as well as having the freedom of occupation that such responsibility suggests. This worked extremely well with the occupants and it meant that the 'admin dept' housed on the first floor, were rarely in the house on their own and were always being reminded of the greater family of which everyone was a part.

The number of people and organisations that used the house grew as time went on and included: A counselling service for young adults, two lunchtime drop-ins for people with mental health issues, the Art Pad besides being home to various small groups, training sessions, courses and a variety of meetings including those associated with the churches and WO. It was also a most convenient venue for groups and organisations based next door at St. Andrew's Church who made regular use of the premises for one-off meetings, or as an over-spill when the church premises ran out of room space.

The benefits of St. Andrew's House as a central administration base for the five churches and Wythenshawe Oasis is explained elsewhere, suffice to say here that the camaraderie between everyone using the house was great fun; just as the exchange of news and information was a source of encouragement that prompted good colleagueship and provided important and much needed meeting-points.

A FUNERAL AT ST. ANDREW'S

It was just a straight forward funeral service, a special one, yes, but are they not all? Except this one had a twist, a message for everyone.

Sid was one of the leaders of the T Dancers. The tea dancers met every Monday and had been a well-established part of New Horizons from its inception and been closely associated with St. Andrew's for years. Before New Horizons came into being and before the premises were transformed, they were simply a regular weekday activity numbering around 80 members. The church hall was their dancing suite with an accessible kitchen. The facilities changed when the premises went through the stages of major alteration and refurbishment with the benefit of becoming much more multi-purpose. The impact of this conversion-cum-modernisation schedule was considerable. Continuing to use the main hall for dancing, they now used the new kitchenette Tea Bar situated at the back of the church for their refreshment breaks. After collecting their drinks, they relaxed amid the soft furnishings in the newly fitted out leisure suite opposite the kitchenette. But as far as the T Dancers were concerned, the church space really came into its own on the occasions they had their parties and grand sit-down meals. Prior to this stylish setting, they had to double-up the hall space involving putting up and taking down of large tables plus the to-ing and fro-ing of all the other sundry components. This whole new setting (not forgetting the up-graded toilets!) was revolutionary and pleasing beyond question.

Sid was greatly admired and cherished by everyone. He was always busy getting everything in order and ready for the dancing. He was a professional. When it came to his funeral arrangements and despite living away from St. Andrew's in an entirely different neighbourhood, the question of venue wasn't even raised; it just seemed not only appropriate but entirely natural that his funeral would be at St. Andrew's. But it is not the case that the service was just held in the church where parties took place and meals were served out of convenience, it was also part and parcel of the Tea Dance day itself with refreshments and dancing in the hall; except on this occasion everything was in honour of the man himself.

The twist became apparent and the message was conveyed in the eulogy when the minister said, "Now you know, now you realise that this church is not the sole domain of other people or the property of the Sunday congregation alone who like us today, worship here. This is Sid's church, Sid who we are commemorating in this funeral service. It is Sid's church not just today but every day particularly Mondays, it is Sid's church, it is your church, it is the church of the Monday T. Dancers. You belong here, you are this church's family and especially when you are here using these premises, the place becomes yours." The minister was able to say this with all the authority he could muster because they loved St. Andrew's and they worked hard alongside the other partner organisations for everything New Horizons stood for. Besides paying their hire fee to Signpost, the partner organisation responsible for the hall, the T. Dancers never faltered in their generosity to the church and in the respect and love of the building and all that it stood for. Saying words from the pulpit no matter how profound they may have been was one thing, the truth of those words was captured in the symbolism of the occasion itself; a symbolism that fused together the spiritual and secular as an expression of the values of the Kingdom of God. Of course it could provide the spiritual setting whenever required and necessary, but the spiritual presence and its relevance was never absent, no more absent than the theological rationale that underpinned the aims and objectives of the T Dance itself.

"This man deserves to have you do this, because he loves our nation and has built our synagogue." (Luke 7:1-10) It is not surprising that this particular story is repeated several times over for two reasons in particular: The principal character in the story not only identifies very closely with particular individuals associated with our Kingdom of God work, but the story itself gives different insights and elucidation concerning the message or messages it is sign-posting; with the consequence that, the different 'messages' relate to our different work situations.

After a short conversation with Jesus in which the Centurion makes a big impression, Jesus not only gave a twist to this story as it evolved, but his accompanying message was as revolutionary as it was stark when he said, "I tell you, I have not found such great faith even in Israel." Jesus credited this centurion with more genuine faith than that of the Jews, who was presumably of no recognisable faith, but a senior officer of an occupying military power as well as being a person under strict orders. In other words, Jesus recognised in the centurion's persona and altruistic endeavours, a spiritual dimension that must have given validity to this man's own integrity. It is from such spiritual sources that a person's principles are formed and a theological base becomes discernible.

There is little difference in the complimentary and commendatory words spoken by Jesus of the centurion, than in his choice of words when speaking about the Kingdom of God. When they are applied to an individual as in this instance to Sid and his team, it means either: The Kingdom of Heaven is already their inheritance, or they are already part of the Kingdom's work. Everything about the T Dance proved its worth as a player in the Kingdom of God, but it was the symbolism of Sid's funeral that struck the message home, just how far they had come in that work and how much further they could still go.

ANECDOTES

The bleeden bailiff

I was organising a narrow boat holiday for a few people and Michael who I knew from his primary school days had secured a crew from his young adult mates. Michael's instructions to me were to go round to his mum's house and she would hand over their monies to me. It wasn't late only about 8 pm but no answer when I knocked. I knocked again, still no answer though I knew she was there, I could tell she was. So for the third time I knocked louder than ever. Eventually she opens the door, "Oh it's you" she said, "I thought you were the bleeden bailiff!"

A Day Out

A mini bus load from our Brownley Green church (the church with the gym and community shop), was on a day out to Rhyl on the North Wales coast. Something happened that made me aware of the contrast between cultures and family nurturing. While others were enjoying the fun and frolics of the local leisure centre's swimming amenities, a mother and extended family originally from Africa were changing into swimming costumes on the beach around the side of the leisure centre, ready to tackle the wind and the waves of the sea. I was struck by the serenity of the children and thought to myself that their acceptance of swimming in the sea and not the swimming pool was noticeably cordial, especially by those so young. Diplomacy reigned in the end, because I managed to persuade their mum to accept the leisure centre's admission costs from a fund I held for such purposes, which meant everyone was able to enjoy the fun and frolics of the swimming pool.

Meanwhile, four or five others (all Brownley Green's community shop helpers) were sitting around a table outside a café larking about as per usual in their convivial manner. Among them was larger-than-life gregarious Pat. Always a hoot, always being teased and always laughing until everyone was laughing, such was Pat. As though he knew its character and was a razor-sharp shot, what must have been a monster of a seagull, offloaded his cargo so that it landed right in the middle of Pat's uncovered head. The laughter was uncontrollable as was Pat's comical and entertaining reaction!

Years later or forward to more current times, I was privileged to attend the university graduation ceremony of one of those girl swimmers from the African family. And a few weeks later there was a bonus, which was to share a meal with her as she told me all about her first weeks as a junior doctor. Boy was I was proud of her, of her family and of our Brownley Green church and people, the delight being I was able to perceive so clearly the rudiments of the Kingdom of God over all those years.

David's deportation

He came from Namibia to see and stay with his sister's family, but as time went on he began to find his place among church, friends and our project work. He became a frequent visitor to our St. Andrew's House and volunteered his services just as much as we appreciated his eagerness to be involved. His visitor's visa eventually ran out and despite several attempts to renew it, each time it was unsuccessful. He cited various reasons why returning to his native Namibia would be dangerous and unpredictable, but he had outstayed his legal rights to stay and exhausted the process of appeal. It was hard for him to leave his sister's family and to cut the ties he had made with the wider church community and the neighbourhood people generally, such was the sense of 'belonging' he was enjoying and valuing, because of its depth of friendship and rapport. The time came when he was required to report to an immigration office every week and I was pleased to accompany him on those occasions and feel a little bit like his protector. All came to a sudden end on the day 'they' came for him, unannounced and with no time for goodbyes; 'they', being the official security officers and the police. There was just time to go to the airport detention centre with his sister and deliver some of his clothes before he boarded the plane that would eventually return him to Namibia. Remonstrating with the officer there, raised in me a strong feeling of injustice because our pleas for a proper goodbye and to see him for the last time were denied. The sense of 'injustice' was more a testimony to our emotions than anything else as no actual unlawfulness had been committed. What is interesting in all of all this, was the bond, the relationship, that sense of belonging to one another. It is as if we had surpassed basic friendliness and comradeship and entered into a 'brother/sister' relationship which is as much spiritual and authentic as it is human and physical. What I call, being a fellow member of the 'family of God.'

CHAPTER 6:
THE KINGDOM OF GOD SEEN THROUGH THE LITURGIES OF THE PEOPLE

T his chapter looks at the wording, style and content of public worship especially for contemporary settings. It gives a graphic account of one particular Sunday morning.

CHURCH SERVICES

I'm the window cleaner who turned up one Sunday morning to clean the windows. Quite a crowd of people were there and something was going on for sure. They were all sitting down except when they sang hymns. I had work to do so I couldn't stop and wait for them to finish or join in, I had windows to clean, so while they carried on doing what they were doing, I carried on cleaning the windows.

Actions speak louder than words

This is a true story just as it happened with imaginary thoughts attributed to the main character.

No-one seemed bothered with me or with what I was doing, but it was while I was doing the big windows on the door opposite the front where everyone was facing, that I noticed something. The man at the front doing all the talking was holding a child - a very young child. After a little while some grown-ups joined him and formed like a circle around something – a bowl of some sort standing on top of a wooden structure. I did actually at that point stop what I was doing because I was intrigued and wondered what was going on. I saw the man cup some water in his hands from the bowl and pour it over the child's face - well, I think it was his face and at the same time he said the child's name followed by other words which you could tell, were carefully chosen. I thought the water would start the child off crying and yelling, but it didn't.

Someone brought a candle, said some words about Jesus and something about the light of the world and then gave the candle to one of the grown-ups standing there. It's what happened next that made me think. The man holding the baby asked some questions and I guess he was looking at the child's mum and dad. They were serious questions – all about loving the child, keeping him safe from evil, saying prayers and being a good example, taking him to church, learning about Jesus and God – all that sort of thing. It was hearing that, that made me think – I wished my mum and dad had promised to do that when I was a kid, things might have turned out differently and life much better for all of us. And then a strange thing came over me. I wanted to run down to the front and like the child's dad say, "Yes I will, I'll do all those things you're asking." But I didn't run down and say that, I couldn't could I? But if ever I'm a dad, I'm going to make sure I do and then me and my kid will have a better life than I had.

Now how should a story like that end? What about, "How shall we say the Kingdom of God is? It is like a man when he was cleaning windows, heard the word of God and afterwards, carried on cleaning the windows except for one thing he promised to himself. If ever he had the chance, he and his would-be child would make sure they find out where the Kingdom was, how to get into it and then never depart from it."

A window cleaner turning up and cleaning the windows while a baptism service was taking place is exactly as it happened. However, the thoughts attributed to the cleaner were imaginary except that if he did actually think in the way the story suggests, it is very possible his thinking would have steered in that direction. To the street-wise person without a background of church or Sunday-School or attendance at church related organisations, services held in churches on Sundays would be alien to him. Given arresting circumstances such as this baptism and the drama, the use of common language, the sincerity, the message it conveyed – all within a spirit of friendship, created a very noticeable impact, a fact that will be illustrated with another true story at the conclusion of this chapter.

Taking into consideration what it means for a church to be a neighbourhood church on a housing estate densely populated with young families drawn from a diverse section of society, means one thing above everything else, the church will need to have its own unique way of doing things and communicating its message. Just as pop concerts in contrast to classical concerts and readers of the Sun Newspaper in contrast to readers of The Times, shows the differences between cultural identities and their respective fraternities, it is crucial that the church has unqualified cultural affinity with the families and people it represents. This requires a close look at the liturgies and worship styles that churches use, asking the question: Does the language, the setting and the fundamental meaning behind church services have that natural and instinctive resonance with the people? An important question because churches should have due regard to their congregation's and their local community's indigenous cultural setting.

The intriguing feature of the window cleaner story is no-one appeared uncomfortable or displeased on the occasion, simply because everyone was singing from the same hymnbook! There were no differences among them.

It is easy to think the sum total of a worship service in church is simply the contents that make up the act of worship itself. Of course the hymns, readings, prayers, sermon and everything that is meant by the 'whole liturgy' are important components, but there are other significant elements without which the assembled community will be short-changed. There's the local community or 'neighbourhood', its ethos, its day-by-day pulse with all the unexpected highs and lows, joys and sorrows people encounter.

There's the whole mix of people with their ethnic backgrounds, their idiosyncrasies, peer groups, parties, not to mention individuals with their personal hopes and aspirations as well as their personal difficulties and heart-aches.

Families with children, especially those who struggle to cope, besides offspring that are lined up for their baptism and the older ones for their weddings.

155

Family members grieving loved ones' who have died and other forms of grief associated with crime and drugs.

'Locals' who have responsibilities drawn from the wide spectrum of volunteers and service personnel, local organisations and their leaders, community clubs, groups and the various self-help agencies with other community based projects.

Local schools, colleges, children's centres, hospitals, clinics and personnel with their various enterprises designed to improve health and welfare; places of employment, job centres, people without employment and citizens advice; the police, social services, probation service, local councillors, not forgetting street pastors.

The backdrop, the ethos, the atmosphere of a place of worship should ideally be created by and portray the many colourful elements where the church is situated in its neighbourhood and wider community. As the people enter the building and the congregation comes together, the distinctive 'culture' should come alive and the job of the liturgy is to enhance that cultural setting in order for the spiritual to be given full expression. But a common language of the people is a key component and that is where most liturgies and liturgical services fall down. Their formal approach, use of old biblical and religious terminology, their long highfalutin phrases without any explanation to their meaning and the sheer 'wordy-ness' of the services, usually means there is no natural rapport with a congregation from a working class background. Congregations thus described and placed in that situation simply go through the motions, they do and say what is expected of them and the great truths hidden in the liturgy remain hidden.

Personalised and specially written liturgies for Baptism and Communion services have been used by the five Wythenshawe churches for many years and with much success. It is interesting that the people who showed most enthusiasm for the services, was by far the people on this housing estate who rarely attended church except on special occasions. Their singing improved the more specially written songs were sung, lighting personalised candles and explaining their significance gave insight into important symbolism, the recitation of a contemporary creedal statement helped towards a personal identity with God and related a personal God to them, appropriate and descriptive wording used for communion and baptism services, together with other forms of participation, made the occasions community events in themselves without losing any of the profundity embedded in the services. Instead of the liturgy being merely a formal service sheet everyone worked through, the liturgy became the people and everything they did! And generally speaking, everyone in those extra-large congregations remained attentive and involved throughout the services.

What follows is a true descriptive account of a Baptism Service which proved to be as arresting and participatory as such services claimed to be.

AN EXTRAORDINARY SUNDAY MORNING

I arrived early to my office at St. Andrew's House which was next to the church, to a surprised greeting - hoards of people as guests of a family whose young child that morning was being baptised. They were one and a half hours early due to a timing error on the invitations! But in no time at all the car park was filling up as was the church entrance hall with people spilling over into the church and passing the newly fitted tea-bar, so I spared no time locating the tea and coffee and anything else I could find including a tin of biscuits. In a matter of minutes two of the guests were busy serving drinks to a queue found in any supermarket. By the time folk from the church community began to arrive, the church was a heaving mass of bodies including excitable children.

I needed to leave my heaving flock to borrow hymnbooks from a couple of the other churches, but on entering the church with the said hymnbooks, I was amazed at the sight I saw. The small coffee tables had children around them with their colouring books, the adults had commandeered the lounge chairs and were making the most of their impromptu break for tea and chat, while other children competed with each other on the football game. And adding to that foray, were mobile and i-phones red hot with text messages and internet info. It could have been Manchester Airport's terminal 4, so cohesive and orderly was the morning's creativity.

Plonking my bags of hymnbooks down, I was confronted in the corridor by two workmen fully equipped with building materials and before a word was spoken, one of the workmen was most keen to tell me about a sketch he had drawn. "You see how the wood-block floor over there is broken and out of place, well I'm doing a feature about wood and while I was here the other day, I drew a sketch of the cross above the altar. There's a connection between the wooden cross and the broken floor blocks because his body was broken on the cross wasn't it?" Before any dialogue could ensue, the other workman explained why they were fitting a new sink unit in one of the rooms used by Studio One; and had already begun plastering up what half an hour before was a door into the room. "Oh I see I said" and then I remembered a phone message from Matthew Studio One's manager and his reference to some building work. "I bet that's what he wanted to talk about" I thought to myself. Excusing myself from further conversation in order to return to the baptism and communion service I was trying to orchestrate, the two workmen dug into their buckets and merrily went on with their plastering.

The next question was from the person with the bread and wine as she was making preparation for communion which was to follow the baptism. "Are all these people having communion as well?" By then the leisure space at the back of the church was full of people and families. "Let's play it by ear" I replied, "and we'll work it out as we go along." More bottles of communion wine were found, people were ushered to their seats and the150 plus congregation were finally going to get their baptism service.

The service soon got into full swing. A church member signalled to me about removing temptation of the large table football game just to be on the safe side, Unnoticed, the little wooden players sporting the red and sky blue shirts quietly made their exit!

"Aspiration" I said, "What do you want this child to aspire to and you his parents, what do you want to aspire to?" And I linked those things that Jesus aspired to with the bread and wine to be used for communion and applied them especially to the family of the child baptised. Before the service was over, a goodly number of families, grown-ups and children joined the church congregation in a dignified if quizzical frame of mind for communion. The interesting thing is that, despite being in church for so long, the whole congregation including the children concentrated on the service without any fuss or distraction. And afterwards there was no stampede to get away either, everyone seemed content just to be there.

This 'extraordinary Sunday morning' was reminiscent of an episode in Jesus' ministry recorded in Luke 14:15, a story known as The Great Feast. One of those listening to Jesus exclaims "Blessed is the man who will eat at the feast in the Kingdom of God." His outburst about feasting in the kingdom of God seemed to be an ideal cue for Jesus to reinforce his message with an interlocking story. Having received excuses from three potential and seemingly 'important' guests invited to a great banquet, invitations then went out to the general public namely; "the poor, the crippled, the blind and the lame" and also to any along the lanes and country roads. End result was, the master's house was full.

This was how Jesus described the Kingdom of God or more precisely, the people who would be within that God-given Kingdom. I see a parallel with the great crowd who came to the baptism. Just as the poor, the crippled, the blind and the lame and others from the byways wouldn't have realised they were entering the Kingdom, it is more than likely that neither would the huge number of guests who had come to the baptism, have realised they too were entering the Kingdom of God, but their attentive and relaxed composure more than suggests they had participated in a 'feast' similar to the one outlined by Jesus.

If church worship first and foremost is designed to help people get onto a personal wave-length with God, it becomes most important therefore that an expression of the spiritual that is within them or is part of them, is experienced or at least acknowledged. "Blessed is the man who will eat at the feast in the kingdom of God" is an animated exclamation that more than suggests someone whose spirituality has suddenly given him insight, enthusiasm and an appreciation of the nearness of the Almighty. And the context on that occasion was clearly not temple or synagogue worship or anything remotely associated with ritual or something devotional, rather it was spoken in the setting of giving hospitality to those most despised who were considered unworthy of any spiritual recognition or value.

Just as Christ was opening up the Kingdom of God to include first and foremost the unconsidered waifs and strays or the 'un-Godly' as some of today's people might say, at the same time and with equal passion he saw the people from the 'streets and alleys of the town, the crippled, the blind and the lame' as representative of the 'neighbourhood' and created what we would call community action.

The families, friends and local people drawn from the neighbourhood who came to the baptism service, likewise on that occasion showed passion, a true sense of community and brought their spirituality into a state of consciousness, thus the place reverberated with the spirituality of the neighbourhood, and the people interacted as a community where God was in the midst of them.

SUNDAY WORSHIP

If church worship is the liturgies of the people, the worship should go a long way to help express and reflect the people's every-day life-style.

If any church denomination can design Sunday Worship to reflect the character of the local neighbourhood and the personalities of its residents, it should be the Methodist Church but not exclusively. Having been taught and trained as ministers in the whys and wherefores of liturgical worship and at the same time appreciating the church's non-conformist background, it should be an instinctive practice to produce good liturgical worship that is of the people and by the people. By that I mean, the main ingredients should encompass the key components and in a complementary order; whilst at the same time giving free licence to impromptu and alternative written and visual material. Such a crafted skill is pretty well an essential requirement on housing estates as testified by the five Wythenshawe churches.

These two examples of liturgical worship, the first one in the setting of Holy Baptism and the second in the setting of Holy Communion, were much used in the five churches and were extremely well received especially by families and people unfamiliar with church services.

SUNDAY WORSHIP WITH HOLY BAPTISM

Introduction and Welcome

Hymn/song:

Lighting of the candles:

> The first candle is lit for children everywhere in the world,
> *May Christ the Light of the World bless them.*
> The second candle is lit for children of this church and
> neighbourhood,
> *May Christ the Light of the World bless them.*
> The third candle is lit for children not at home with their parents,
> *May Christ the Light of the World bless them.*
> The fourth candle is lit for children who are unwell and poorly,
> *May Christ the Light of the World bless them.*

The fifth candle is lit for the child of this baptism today,
May Christ the Light of the World give his blessing.

Our prayers:

Christ Jesus,
You grew up at Nazareth with your parents
learning as much as you could about God.
You learnt from your parents and teachers
as much as you could about the world.
You learnt from your own baptism in the river
that it was time to begin your great work.

We say this prayer together:

Dear God,
Come and be our guest today,
Come in Jesus we pray.
Come in a form we can understand,
Come so we all can make a stand.
Come in your forgiving love,
Come and give us all a shove.

A chant is sung:

A passage from the Bible is read:

Hymn/song:

It is the baptism of the Father, the Creator,
The one who has breathed life into this child that we seek

It is the baptism of the Son, Jesus the Christ,
Friend of all people then and now, that we seek.

It is the baptism of the Spirit, that mystical presence of God,
Unseen yet everywhere, that we seek.

As we come together Lord and obey your call to baptise,
Lord Jesus, we remember you and believe in you.

As we share this child's baptism, we pray for your blessing,
Lord Jesus, we remember you and believe in you.

As we see the love of this child's parents and family,
Lord Jesus, we remember you and believe in you.

As we hear promises made by this child's family, friends and church,
Lord Jesus, we remember you and believe in you.

As we join in the worship of all believers,
Lord Jesus, baptize us in your love,
Inspire us with your courage,
And move us by your presence.

Let us say this creedal statement as a basis of our belief in God:

We believe in God
Creator and architect of the world,
From solar systems to computers,
From eclipses of the sun to fun loving pets,
Of all that has been and all that is to be,
God of life, God of the after-life,
We believe in God.

We believe in Jesus,
Who wore the human face of God,
Welcomed the children,
Healed the sick,
Blessed the people
And opened up to everyone the new kingdom of God.
We believe in Jesus,

We believe in the Holy Spirit,
Who enables God to be everywhere,
Unseen, unheard, often unknown.
The catalyst of every prayer,
The enthusiasm of every Christian,
The divine spark of every soul.
We believe in the Holy Spirit.

Water, Font and Candle are made ready -

The Baptism:

> "...I baptise you in the name of God,
> Father, Son and Holy Spirit."

> Child of God, child of love, you are creation's gift of life.
> In you God's image is revealed and through you humanity is reborn.

> *Through the Sacrament of Holy Baptism,*
> *We receive you into the Congregation of Christ's People.*

The Baptism Candle:

> This is a sign for you now belong to Christ the Light of the World,
> Let your light shine, that everyone may see God in your life.

> *The Lord bless you and keep you;*
> *The Lord make his face to shine upon you,*
> *and be gracious unto you;*
> *The Lord lift up his countenance upon you, and give you peace.*

The Parents -

> Will you surround this child with true love and affection,
> And nurture him/her in the Christian Faith,
> keeping him/her safe from harm?
> *Yes I will.*

> Will you acquire the right life-style so that your words, prayers
> And deeds are a good example to this child?
> *Yes I will.*

> Will you engage this child in Christian worship and teaching,
> That he/she may choose to make his/her own
> confession of faith?
> *Yes I will.*

The Godparents -

> Will you take a keen and friendly interest in this child,
> Always being there when needed,

And will you give lots of support to his/her mum and dad?
Yes I will.

Hymn/song

Some thoughts about God -

Prayer blessings:

Let us pray for friends and families...
Lord, bless these people.
In the name of Christ, bless everyone.

Let us pray for people who are unwell...
Lord, bless these people.
In the name of Christ, bless everyone.

Let us pray for people who work with children...
Lord, bless these people.
In the name of Christ, bless everyone.

Let us pray for people in the world...
Lord, bless these people.
In the name of Christ, bless everyone.

Let us pray for this church...
Lord, bless these people.
In the name of Christ, bless everyone.

Amen.

Notices and Offering:

Hymn/song

Blessing:

There is nothing more to be said or done.
Everything has been said and done to the glory of God.
Go from this place in peace and come back to this place in love.
In the name of God we will.
God bless you today, tomorrow and forever more.
Amen

(The above was the liturgy that was used on that extraordinary Sunday morning at St. Andrew's Church)

HOLY COMMUNION IN THE SETTING OF SUNDAY WORSHIP

Let us pray,

Lord our God,
As we come together as one community among many
May the spirit of Christ be truly present with us and in us,
That inspired by his teaching,
Our worship shall:
> **Sing your praise,**
> **Increase our faith,**
> **Strengthen our community**
> **And establish your kingdom on earth.**

Prayers continue...

The Lord's Prayer:
Our Father...

Let us say our creedal statement:

God is the God of all that has been, and all that is to be.
God is God of all life and life after death we call heaven.

We believe God created the world and made us all in his image,
and that everyone and everything should be seen to be holy and treated with respect.

Jesus is God in human form as the Bible makes clear.
He lived he worked and died for people everywhere.

We believe in what Jesus taught, what he did and how he lived,
and in the Christian response to follow him.

The Holy Spirit is like air, it is everywhere but never seen.
It gives us ideas, encouragement and confidence in things we do.

We believe the Holy Spirit is there when we say prayers,
when we say sorry,

and when we forgive someone, that is the way
God gives his blessing.

It was you O Lord who formed our inward parts;
You knitted them together in our mother's womb.
Our frame was not hidden from you,
When we were made in the secret place.

Let us apologise to God for personal failures and failings:

Search us, O God, and know our hearts;
Challenge us and know our thoughts.
See if there is any way we are impaired,
And lead us all in the way that is everlasting.

The spirit of community must have been as strong as it was real
when Jesus was with his disciples for their last supper together.
Pointing to the bread, Jesus blessed it and gave some to his disciples
saying the words: 'Take, eat. This is my body given for you.
Do this in remembrance of me.'
Passing the wine round and having given thanks, he said,
'Drink from it all of you, this is my blood of the new covenant,
poured out for you and for people everywhere.
Do this also in remembrance of me.'

Lord my God,
Bless my hands that are receiving these holy gifts,
my soul that is being fed this spiritual food.
Bless my thoughts that remind me of your life-giving stories,
my body with your becalming presence.
Bless my hopes, my dreams, my aspirations
and the person I am with your words of encouragement.

Bread and Wine are shared...

Here through the sharing of bread and wine,
We have renewed our journey with Christ
and identified ourselves with his kingdom.

Here in this Holy Communion,
We have renewed our love with one another
and identified ourselves with everything our community stands for.

Here, in this act of solidarity,
We have accepted the sacrificial life to which we are called,
and commit ourselves to a life of justice and peace for everyone.

The Blessing:
Go now because our time together is over.
Love Christ and do the things he has done.

We will dream dreams and go with our hopes for his kingdom.

The Lord Jesus bless you this day and every day,
Until his kingdom is fulfilled.
Amen.

Those two liturgies simply illustrate the way a little creativity together with a common language and style; can be a contemporary presentation without losing the integrity of liturgical worship.

ANECDOTES:

Mo's crew and Ann Summers

When Brownley Green's charity shop ran out of stock of new clothes because the out of date catalogue supply had dried up; me, Mo and three others from the shop set off in search of new suppliers. We went to the Trafford Centre in Greater Manchester where there are numerous stores and shopping outlets. With our spiel to store managers well-rehearsed, we went from one to another doing our best to demonstrate the urgency of our need and our commitment to the people we serve. There was one store I saw looming up as we strolled along the hallway; it was Ann Summers and I just couldn't resist 'frog-marching' my loyal band into it. With my shoulder giving a gentle shove, I guided them into the all feminine-stocked shop. (Ann Summers specialises in provocative feminine lingerie). Thinking this was going to give us a bit of a reprieve from being seriously minded and at the same time create a 'lighter' moment with a bit of embarrassment thrown in, I was somewhat mistaken! The joke was thrown back on me when the nature of the store made not an iota of difference to my compatriots and instead, they pursued their task just the same by perusing the merchandise in the same diligent way as they did in all the other stores. This meant of course, it was me who found himself, explaining to the manager the reason for our visitation whilst at the same time, wanting to exit the place as soon as I could! And, no we didn't leave the store with armfuls of out of date stock.

He's a Dick

It was just a customary visit to say hello to a daughter of a church family and her partner who had recently moved to a house they could call their own. Unlike other greetings on the doorstep, on opening the door on this occasion and seeing me standing there she said, "Oh David not now, I'm having a big row with Paul, he's a dick."

Michael's Narrow Boat

The plan was to use Michael's mates as crew for both narrow boats and have mixed ages on both crafts. After a temporary mooring-up on the first day to buy essential supplies, Michael's boat with all his mates on board set off before mine but there was no panic because we were both cruising along the same canal and would eventually meet up. Unfortunately there was a turning on the left which unknown to me and my ship's company, Michael's boat had taken. And so throughout the entire time 'at sea' the two boats went their separate ways not helped by intermittent mobile signals making communication erratic and confusing. When we finally met up on the last evening before returning the boats to the canal basin, all hell was let lose. Not only had the passengers who were not Michael's mates had to accept an alternative voyage, they had to endure very unsavoury behaviour and suspect smoking. With Michael and his crew lined up on the embankment where they were moored, they had to face a lecture from me in which I was prosecution, judge and jury. Two revealing details emerged. The first was my own shortcomings in failing to manage the whole expedition properly and competently, laying all the blame for what happened on the shoulders of Michael and his mates. The second detail was the way Michael and his mates accepted their part in the fiasco and were genuinely sorry. I was concerned my lecture and its aftermath may have impaired my relationship with Michael; a relationship that had grown and matured over the years. I knew how important and auspicious that relationship with Michael had been but fortunately it was not impaired and was even stronger than before.

CHAPTER 7:
THE KINGDOM OF GOD SEEN THROUGH PORTRAITS OF UNFORGETTABLE PEOPLE

"I could jump over the moon"

The six stories in this chapter draw special attention to the overriding message they convey. Besides their underlying stories, each story reveals the sort of message that is often obscured but contains an unassailable truth.

A CHANCE CONVERSATION

Bill was sitting on the bus on his way to town and just by chance a conversation ensued with the lady passenger next to him. With the preliminaries brief as they were over, Bill in his friendly manner began speaking about his church and more precisely, about the project work being undertaken by all five churches.

Bill and his wife Barbara have been members of Northenden church for donkey's years and became keen advocates (almost like missionaries) of the enterprises associated with their church and not least with the whole Kingdom of God initiative throughout the five churches.

It is unknown to me how the conversation navigated itself to a particular conundrum Wythenshawe Oasis were trying to address, but Bill was clearly articulating it to his fellow passenger. He was telling her about the role of Wythenshawe Oasis within the whole set-up and the need for a treasurer with the expertise to oversee the finances and play a key part in raising funds. Knowing Bill, I could quite imagine him asking his co-passenger if she herself had such skills to be a treasurer, but that's only my presumption because, his fellow passenger in question did reveal to Bill that her daughter was an accountant with her own accountancy business. Before reaching their journey's end and saying their goodbyes, the animated conversation concluded by passing on the daughter's details to Bill.

The daughter's name was Sarah and after Bill passed on her details to me, I visited Sarah and her family in their home; and in no time at all Sarah became treasurer of Wythenshawe Oasis. Dispensing with the idea of naming the usual fees, Sarah took up the position and in time, did indeed play a full and important part in raising substantial funds as well as raising the profile of Wythenshawe Oasis generally and specifically in relation to its professional outreach to funding bodies and potential partners.

There was also a chance conversation between someone called Philip and an Ethiopian. It begins: "Now an angel of the Lord said to Philip, 'Go south to the road, the desert road that goes down from Jerusalem to Gaza.' So he started out and on his way he met an Ethiopian..." "...Do you understand what you are reading?" Philip asked. "But the Ethiopian did not understand, so he invited Philip to come and sit with him. Philip then began explaining to the Ethiopian what the passage of scripture he was reading meant; and told him about Jesus and about the good news associated with Jesus..." "...As they travelled along the road, they came to some water and the Ethiopian said, 'Look here is water, why shouldn't I be baptised?' "And he gave orders to stop the chariot. Then both Philip and the Ethiopian went down into the water and Philip baptised him."

This chance encounter and conversation was in the early days after Christ's resurrection and ascension and at a time when the disciples were beginning to take on the role of missionaries. There is no doubt that the Ethiopian was a sincere man, devout even in that he was seeking spiritual values with possibly a morality or code of ethics by which he could live. By profession he was the chancellor of the exchequer of a titled queen of Ethiopia in other words, his business was finance, a treasurer even. Intrigued as he was with the Isaiah passage he was reading made him either someone looking towards adopting Judaism as his religion or maybe becoming so closely associated with the Jewish Faith that he would adhere to the faith's principles. Both options point to this man seeking the Christ in Isaiah 53 which was unquestionably confirmed in his desire for baptism.

As time went on and Wythenshawe Oasis did its job of raising funds for the churches project work, Sarah herself with her family identified with the spiritual values and core beliefs underpinning the whole network of kingdom of God activities by requesting that she and her child be baptised. And as in the story about the Ethiopian, she and her child's baptisms duly took place at our Lawton Moor Church.

None of us had a monopoly when, where or how the Kingdom of God would manifest itself, our responsibility was to create opportunities and go where thy led us. If that was on a bus innocently talking to someone, sitting in someone's living room explaining what it's all about, each person using their skills and expertise for the common good, or standing around a font and being baptised; what became essential was always to use discernment and never miss the opportunity when it came, even a chance conversation.

The story of Philip and the Ethiopian is found in Acts of the Apostles 8: 26-40.

The Isaiah passage the Ethiopian was reading was from Isaiah 53: 1-12.

MARY AND MARTHA

These true stories of two Wythenshawe people are presented in the personalities of Mary and Martha, the sisters Jesus visited on his travels. To gain the most out of the stories, read about Mary and Martha in Luke 10: 38-42.

Mary is in her nineties and she has lived on her own since her sister died many years ago. Her incapacity seriously restricts her mobility to the extent she can only just get from one room to another, so she is at home all the time. In her younger days, Mary and her sister played a full and active part in the life of their church and were always involved doing this, that, and the other for and on behalf of the local community. All she is able to do now is sit and talk and be hospitable to visitors, which she does with grace and charm. When she is visited by her church minister, she will repeatedly ask him a recurring question; "What now is the purpose for my life? I have always been told that God has a purpose for us, but what purpose is there for me now? I can't do anything or go anywhere except sit here so what is the answer, what purpose is there for me?"

Martha is in her early eighties, she has had six children and two of the boys who are now in their fifties are still living with her. There was a particular occasion when she recalled to her minister a very personal and tragic part of her family history. The conversation occurred the morning after the night before because 'last evening', Martha as a mother was faced with one of those impossible situations. The minister had given Martha a lift home in his car and it was whilst parked outside her house that she recalled the nightmare of the evening before.

Her two sons don't get on, they are always arguing, always fighting, always making day-to-day family life extremely difficult. One of the sons is an alcoholic and the other one is a drug addict which means both of them are very rarely free from the influence of their addictions. Following a particularly nasty argument between them and after quite bizarre behaviour, the son on drugs climbed a tree and was threatening to kill himself. The only thing Martha felt she could do in that situation was to call the police and she knew that by so doing she would to all intents and purposes, be sectioning him under the Mental Health Act, sectioning her own son and that is what happened.

She then continued the conversation and recalled some other painful memories, the daughter who was murdered by the daughter's own husband and another daughter who died from cancer. And this mother who has had to endure so much is only slight, can't be more than seven or eight stone and not altogether a well person either, yet she still has to endure family upheaval. Despite all that and the distress it causes, the only hint of a negative comment from this lady, is when she refers to her age and says she feels a bit too old to be coping with the strain and stress of these two middle-aged sons. Notwithstanding her family commitments, this person is also the life and soul of the local community shop where she works as a volunteer. And in that volunteering role she is always sharing her much loved humour as well as showing sensitivity and empathy to those around her with their own trials and tribulations.

Whilst Mary keeps asking for an answer to her question about a purpose for her life, Martha without asking the question spends so much of her time fulfilling a purpose she wishes would become superfluous. The point is, known or unknown to them they are both fulfilling a purpose that is truly vocational in nature, because they are playing their part, making their contribution to the on-going work and business of the Kingdom of God.

In this true story and despite feeling her age and incapacities, the character of Mary draws on her life-long experience and knowledge and uses them in conversation with her visitors and in the regular cycle of her prayers. By so doing she is interesting herself in the day-to-day affairs of life and experience, especially in regards to her fellow conversationalist compatriot as and when those encounters take place. And therein lay all the symbolism of two pilgrims on a shared pilgrimage, not dissimilar at all with the conversation between Jesus and Mary when he called by on his way to Jerusalem.

The character of Martha on the other hand in this story is always busying herself with one thing or another. And whether it is out of necessity as with her two middle-aged sons, or out of choice as when she is at the community shop, this person is scrupulously attentive and ever faithful to the message of the Kingdom, especially in its speaking of self-denial and taking up the cross.

Both of these characters are living prayers in their own right, whether the prayers are read from a book, said in the lighting of a candle, spoken out loud as in a conversation or expressed in the way they go about their lives; their 'living prayer' keeps them in touch and engaged in the world around them, in relationships of spiritual depth and in the Kingdom of God which sustains all things.

THE MAN WHOSE LIFE WAS TURNED AROUND

This is a little test, see if you can answer it. What was the main character in one of Jesus' parables which ends with these words: "He was dead and is alive again; he was lost and is found, and that is why we had to celebrate and be glad." The words of Jesus refer to the homecoming of someone whose life was turned around and it is found in Luke 15:11-32. This story, also of a man, whose life was turned around, begins when he was on his way to the very place where that dramatic change occurred. The story begins with the man's own words:

"I can't thank you enough for what you have done because you wouldn't believe the difference it has made to my life. It has changed everything and it is fantastic. I don't just have something to do these days; I have somewhere I can go and feel at home and something to live for. I really can't thank you enough, it is wonderful."

His words were like a pronouncement as he steered his wheelchair in my direction. It was obvious by his fast spoken words that he wanted to tell me something and wasn't going to miss this opportunity. Having made sure he was speaking to the right person, he then proceeded to say one thank you after another and just couldn't stop showing his appreciation.

He was one of the art students from Studio One, the organisation that specialised in art based activities as described in the account of Studio One's work under the project name of 'New Horizons'. The reason for this person's state of euphoria and eagerness to show appreciation was simple; a ramp had been built at Studio One's entrance and he was now able to gain access without the usual commotion and difficulty.

What he didn't know was that the ramp was built before the funding for it had been secured, and as no funding body would even consider retrospective payment, the ramp's costs were finally met from someone's personal donation and reimbursed later by the church. The point is the ramp had a huge effect as it changed the perspective of the place and not just by the accessibility it gave, but by the sheer weight of positive feelings now enjoyed by those from the world of disabilities. They felt they truly belonged, that everyone was accommodated on equal terms and a sense of commonality of spirit and purpose resonated around the whole place. Actually, it wasn't only a ramp that had been put into place, interior doors of several rooms had also been enlarged for wheelchair access.

At first, his acclamation conveying much gratitude appeared over the top. It was only a ramp, but that was out of ignorance because more was to be discerned. As highlighted under 'New Horizons' in chapter 4, the whole vision behind Studio One was to create a working environment entirely conducive for people too often left on the margins of society because of their special needs and for people who feel valueless to themselves and to society generally.

With the specialist nature of Studio One's work, its equipment, technical know-how and skills to match and a striving to meet more and more people's needs, it is not surprising that more individuals from the harsh world of abandonment were accommodated. And it is most likely the case that the person so pleased with the newly installed ramp might also have represented many lost souls who have low self-esteem and feel personally demoralised, for whom the ramp symbolised positivity over negativity.

One person biding his time to show unfettered appreciation is reminiscent of another story told by Jesus in Luke 17:12-19. In this story, a man who had been cured of his leprosy, returned to Jesus with undiluted thanksgiving and appreciation. And as in that story of the healing of the ten with leprosy despite only one out of the ten showed appreciation, the outward expression of joy over the ramp was similarly by someone whose protestations were not going to be restrained. Indeed, he was himself a spokesperson for many more who were similarly blessed and whose faith can be described as a life-changing experience.

Trying as I did to indicate to the man that the part I played in the process was simply to find the funds, while others made sure it happened by building the ramp and widening the doors. He replied, "Ah, it's more than that to me", it's turned my life around, do you have any idea what that is like?"

The words of Jesus quoted at the beginning: "He was dead and is alive again; he was lost and is found, and that is why we had to celebrate and be glad," refer to a life that was turned around, the same words used by the man in the wheelchair who couldn't say thank you enough, because his life had likewise been turned around.

ZACCHAEUS & BRIGHT HOUSE

These Wythenshawe people are associated with the story of Zacchaeus found in Luke 19: 1-10.

Zacchaeus was doing nothing wrong collecting the people's taxes that was his work and he probably did it diligently and kept all his records up to date. It was not his fault that his employer and the peoples' government were the notorious Roman overlords. Someone had to be employed to receive the taxes and Zacchaeus himself would have needed a job. Likewise these days, a manager at one of the notorious Bright House Stores could claim he was not default in any way, just doing his job as he told his inquisitor, because as he explained, he like everyone else at the end of the day needs to take home a pay packet. But that is as far as the innocence of these two men goes. (Bright House stores sell furniture, a wide range of electrical goods and some general household requisites and it is commonly known that their customers are often people on low incomes, strapped for cash and take advantage of Bright House's buy on credit finance; only to find the interest rate rockets up to unaffordable rates in a matter of days).

A call to the church minister from the manager at the Bright House and his subsequent meeting with him begins this story, but actually the sad tale of events began long before any involvement by the minister. Like the multitudes of tax payers in Zacchaeus's day, this husband and wife if only they knew it, were more than mere customers of the Bright House store; they were legally binding debtors to them. Both had fairly severe learning difficulties and were vulnerable to the commercial company's powers of seduction. In this instance they thought they had bought items of furniture; a television and DVD recorder outright. Instead they had signed a contract in which they promised to pay the creditor (Bright House), the money as agreed for the house-hold items including the cost of the ever rising interest rates. The initial affordable rate of re-payment including interest was payable. What this couple did not realise was the speed with which the interest on their loan would increase. In just a matter of weeks the interest had risen to a figure totally beyond their means to pay. It was fast approaching 94.7% APR (annual percentage rate). With hundreds of £s owing and, would very soon be in the thousands, was sufficient concern for the Bright House manager to contact the person who had agreed to act as surety - the church minister.

Only the minister had not made any such agreement at all with them, but on the other hand he did think it providential at this desperate stage to be drawn into the equation. In no time at all the minister saw himself as advocate to the husband and wife and as litigator to the Bright House manager. Several important facts came to light in the ensuing inquiry and dialogue that was initiated by the minister. No contact at all with the minister by Bright House to act as surety was even attempted. There was no serious inquiry at all made to the husband and wife concerning their financial situation. Despite the husband and wife's obvious and recognisable learning difficulties, no appreciation of their limited circumstances was even remotely considered. Detailed explanation of the contract to a point of the husband and wife understanding something of the basics of the agreement they were signing was never given. The ethos of the store, the sales pitch, the vulnerability of the husband and wife to fall foul to the pressure of thinking they could have more and more possessions, all converged to create gross exploitation and robbery to an inoffensive couple.

The corruption of tax collector Zacchaeus was self-made and whether or not he was following convention and the customs of fellow employees, did not lessen in the slightest the serious exploitation and robbery of the power-less he lorded over. Similarly, the Bright House manager in the way he did not execute his legitimate managerial duties and responsibilities to the vulnerable husband and wife, showed contempt and ridicule towards those he also lorded over. The salvation that came to the home of Zacchaeus on the day he was visited by Jesus extended the values of the Kingdom of God to no less than the power-less tax payers of the day. The same applied to the part played by the minister by confronting the manager of the Bright House store and procuring a just settlement that too, was due no less to the authority invested in the principles and values of the Kingdom of God itself.

If the principal characters of these two stories was merely: Zacchaeus and the husband and wife, it will mean that only a fraction of the message Jesus was seeking to make known would have been grasped. As with most messianic parabolic teaching and incidents drawn from every-day life, it is necessary to grasp the comprehensiveness of the whole chronicle being told. Jesus used the story to exhort a new morality and to live by a new code of ethics in the belief that ever widening communities of people will be able to live according to the justice that is shown to them. That Zacchaeus and the Bright House manager needed to turn their lives around to one of integrity is unquestioned, but most important is the greater effect upon swathes of people exploited and robbed represented in this instance by the husband and wife with the learning difficulties.

It is when looking through the eyes of the Kingdom of God, that something of the scope and huge potential for Christian witness, service and ministry becomes truly apparent because it includes everyone everywhere, without distinction, circumstances or favour. If the minister in the story was not known to the husband and wife and if the minister was not embracing all people without distinction in his ministerial work, how would salvation have come to the home of the exploited and vulnerable being robbed by the Bright House store? But what arouses particular interest, are the reasons why the manager approached the minister in the first place; he erroneously thought as guarantor, the minister would help produce the cash or reduce the ever increasing debt. Instead, the minister made clear to the manager what happens when innocent vulnerable people misunderstand the consequences of enticing offers, and the responsibility that is placed on managers of establishments like this one.

The concept of the Kingdom of God can be contemplated in both an imaginary way and at the same time in a real way. The imaginary way is 'seeing' individuals and groups of people interacting with one another as they give and receive their attentiveness freely and without hindrance and at the same time, more and more people being drawn into such mutually beneficial communities that are totally safe even for the most vulnerable. The real way is seeing and respecting all people as God's people, part and parcel of the great international family of God, of equal worth and purpose and comprising communities where there are no boundaries or demarcation lines, or anything that would make a distinction between one person and another.

Communities where all are members by virtue of being born in the image of God which, itself invalidates any form of enrolment and encourages collective responsibility and a shared pilgrimage. It is this concept that churches in particular need to embrace, for by so doing they will be less introspective and more outward looking which was Christ's spoken appeal to Zacchaeus and just as important, it was also his unspoken appeal to the vast crowd of onlookers outside. Therefore, it can be rightly claimed, that the blessings of the Kingdom of God were as freely accessible to the husband and wife in the Bright House story as they were to the Bright House manager himself and for a period of time regardless of how brief that time might have been, all three characters were indeed drawn into the workings and blessings of no less than the Kingdom of God itself.

THE LADY WHO COULD JUMP OVER THE MOON

Sitting on a chair outside the treatment room was an elderly lady with all the symptoms of arthritis. When asked if she required anything she politely answered, "No thank you, I'm just waiting to see the therapist." This was very soon after offering alternative therapies had begun operating, at the church whose project was to provide services and pastoral care to the over 50s.

The minister's vestry had already been converted into a fully equipped treatment room, (prayers with the preacher on Sundays were now surrounded by massage oils, towels, treatment couch and the like) and funding for the expensive treatment couch plus other equipment was raised by the church's volunteer project manager, supported by Wythenshawe Oasis as the churches' combined charity.

A week or two had passed before seeing the elderly lady again as she was coming into church, shuffling along the best way she could, such was the severity of her arthritic bones. When asked how the therapy had gone down, without pausing for a second, her face lit up and her voice rang out, "It was wonderful, I could jump over the moon!" She then continued in her shuffling way towards the treatment room. Seeing the instant joy on the lady's face and her new found excitement was like an instant play-back of people's encounters with Jesus and on this occasion and with as much verve, it suddenly brought to life these lines of Charles Wesley:

"Hear him, ye deaf; his praise, ye dumb,
Your loosened tongues employ;
Ye blind, behold your Saviour come;
And leap, ye lame, for joy!"

(From the hymn: O for a thousand tongues to sing)

As time went on, this person joined fellow contemporaries by coming regularly to meetings at the centre where other services and consultations tailor-made for an ageing clientele were also available. And in time the spirit of together-ness, comradeship and mutual support fostered the beginnings of a therapeutic community, a community that drew people together from different activities and which grew in strength and purpose.

Such weekly meetings, attended by professional trainers of the various task orientated sessions and not least by church volunteer helpers themselves, far exceeded the role of the familiar church's fellowship groups. This new therapeutic community with Kingdom of God written all over it gave a true sense of equality, personal assurance and an open-ness to all-comers that legitimised its place in that Kingdom. An account of the developing project this story alludes to; features under the title of 'Healthy Living Network' in chapter 4.

TWO SISTERS & THE FAITH OF A GENTILE WOMAN

Go to Mark 7: 24-30 for the accompanying passage associated with this story of the two sisters.

They came to Wythenshawe seeking asylum after leaving their native Eritrea and their father with whom they lived for a period of time in South Africa. The older one was in her twenties and her younger sister just fourteen. Initial contact with them was through one of the Wythenshawe churches which they began attending having been brought up Christian back home. They went through the usual process for people seeking asylum and were finally assigned a 'council house' under the auspices of a housing association. Whilst the younger sister attended secondary school, her older sibling sought work and through her cleaning jobs they made ends meet and paid their way.

The younger one of the two was conscientious, mature for her age, always willing to volunteer her help and worked hard at school. She had a good command of English, good social skills, accepted responsibilities without question and was always cheery and polite. Her older sister was unquestionably hard working, loyal, always gracious, meticulous carrying out duties assigned to her, genuinely grateful for any consideration or kindness shown to them, outrageously generous and truly humble.

By their very nature, it was always a privilege to be in their company, but because of their personal circumstances it was always important, too, to be of assistance to them as and when necessary.

One such opportunity arose when something that had been happening at one of the elder sister's workplaces. Her manager had for some time been demanding a considerable weekly sum of money from her and if she didn't hand it over she would lose her job. It was also the case that as time went on, the company was appointing only Filipinos to be cleaners, making the conditions increasingly difficult for her. It was obvious that this was to make sure she would leave her employment. Knowing her as a person of integrity and the reliance both sisters had upon her earnings (the younger sister being a sibling and not a daughter meant there was no entitlement for the usual state benefits), the minister offered to represent her and to see that justice was done. In the event she deemed to simply leave that employment and double her efforts finding new work despite efforts to persuade her otherwise.

Another opportunity arose over letters and other correspondence she had been receiving. Being an asylum seeker and given entitlement to remain in the U.K. meant the sisters would receive official papers and correspondence from a number of agencies and authorities. These would range from government departments and taxation authorities, to housing associations and job centres. Not surprisingly when different pieces of correspondence got a bit mixed up, the worried expression would be etched on her face, with the familiar signs of fear and panic. Everything was always sorted and found to be above board, something easy for church/project admin staff to resolve, but something formidable and immensely problematic for the two sisters.

A further concern coming out of the blue and finding its way on top of the other anxieties was the bedroom tax as it became known. At first, there was speculation that vulnerable residents would be protected and saved from paying the tax and if that was not the case, then they would be able to move to accommodation with fewer bedrooms. The two sisters occupied a 3-bedroom house and didn't require the third bedroom.

The dimension of the sister's third bedroom was 203cm x 260cm and the smallness of the room made it a non-starter for an occupant. Despite extensive inquiries and form filling to enable the sisters to be transferred to a two-bedroom dwelling and for all the rhetoric about being safeguarded from the said tax, they just had to work even harder at finding more work, so they could pay the extra cost incurred because of the third bedroom, despite it being of little practical use to themselves or to a third party.

About the same time a male resident made himself known. He wanted to know how he could go about finding someone to occupy his spare bedroom as he wouldn't be able to afford to pay the bedroom tax. And this man had clearly done his homework because his calculations were correct; he would not be able to afford the extra cost. His attempts to find answers to queries about finding a tenant drew a blank. The Housing Association, Local Authority, Job Centre, Citizens Advice, Social Services all failed to offer helpful advice. The problem remained; just how would anyone go about finding a bedroom tenant candidate that would fit into their particular family and be of no risk?

The exploitation of the vulnerable was as much a cause of concern in biblical times as it is in these. A study of the Gentile Woman in Mark 7:24 who went to Jesus to ask him to cast a demon out of her possessed daughter, is revealing. The main focus of attention instead of being on the daughter is in fact concentrated on the woman, the daughter's mother, and the nature of the exploitation she is enduring is because of her nationality. Even the way distinction is made between the Jews and the non-Jews highlights the prejudicial attitude that was common towards non-Jews. It's a form of exploitation that is intended to remind the non-Jew that they are inferior, the underdog and the mere fact the woman approached Jesus in person, was a pretty bold thing to do in itself.

The terminology used in the short conversation between the woman and Jesus alludes to that accepted difference between Jews and non-Jews, the 'children' being the Jews and the 'dogs' being the non-Jews or Gentiles. The difference between the two peoples is accentuated when Jesus tells the woman first and foremost, he should feed the children (the Jews) and even the scraps from the children's bread should not be thrown to the dogs (non-Jews). This is sort of coded language to explain that the Messiah is the agent of Israel's God as foretold by the prophets over centuries and therefore it is the children of Israel who have legitimate claim on him. But there is a twist and it comes after the woman's reply.

By granting her request and healing the daughter of her possession, Jesus moves the goal-posts and acknowledges that his Messianic status is no longer confined to the Jews but is available to the non-Jewish world also. But it is also startlingly clear that this was prompted because of the response from the child's mother. Addressing Jesus as 'Lord' indicates her faith in him and her belief in his divinity. Suggesting to Jesus that left-overs that are usually offered to the dogs under the table, is in fact pointing out that the relationship of 'dog' may be a much weaker kinship than that of the 'children', nevertheless you cannot deny its authenticity, weak though it maybe, it is a proper relationship. That was nothing less than insight by the woman of the highest order. Moving the goal-posts as Jesus did, healing the daughter as he did and all because of the faith and belief of the non-Jewish woman is demonstrative of God's Kingdom that Jesus was physically, symbolically, spiritually and emotionally establishing.

A comparison between the non-Jewish woman and the older sister in the story above is intriguing:

- They both had cultural backgrounds different from the status-quo.
- They had a faith that was very important to them.
- They showed a high level of trust in those who cared about them.
- They lived according to their principles.
- They were content in their ordinariness.
- Their humility was as natural as their graciousness.
- Their courage came from their self-esteem.
- They were valued for the individuals they were.
- They shared a universal equality.
- They were selfless in motive and practice.
- They were vulnerable to rumour, deceit, fraud and treachery.
- They were people of integrity.
- They both were prey to exploitation.
- They both have their place in the Kingdom of God.

Similar to the weave-like shape and pattern of a decorative tapestry, the Kingdom of God wove its way in and out all these personal profiles; on the one hand just ordinary people but on closer examination, ordinary people who reveal extraordinary facts. It was the guiding principle into which so much faith and trust was invested and a new future for the church and for partner organisation alike was discovered. The whole experience multiplied, over and over again with the other churches and partner organisations, is indicative of the way collaborative working today, can be similar to what Jesus described in his day, as being the work of the Kingdom of God.

CHAPTER 8:
UPS AND DOWNS

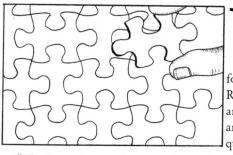

U ps and downs, covers a range of subjects from difficulties and setbacks, ways and means of forming partners and raising funds. Resolving issues and general ways and means of achieving everything are covered in frequently asked questions.

"The last piece and – completion"

DIFFICULTIES AND SETBACKS

Brownley Green's Cabins Aflame

Of the five churches, it is Brownley Green's that is situated in the middle of the estate and regarded as the toughest and most hardnosed area of the domain, though that has to be qualified due to all the law abiding and amiable tenants who are clearly in the majority. In the church grounds next to the church hall were two portacabins. One was used by Copperdale Trust as a temporary store for food collected from supermarkets and housed many refrigerated cabinets; the food subsequently being distributed to people and outlets in need. The second cabin was the church's charity shop selling clothes, knick-knacks and bric-a-brac. One night both cabins were burnt down. The cause of the fires was never known but arson was the most likely and rumours were rife. Nothing could be done, the cabins were a wreck, their smouldering contents of no value and such a setback as it was, had to be faced. To make matters worse, it was my brief to make sure the two cabins were properly insured, something I was always intending to do but hadn't quite got round to that bit of administration. Accepting but not despairing at the seemingly pessimistic situation and not just by me but by everyone at Brownley Green, we bashed on just as we always did, by showing an amazing positive approach to difficulties and crises. I got in touch with Methodist Insurance and I clearly remember that my call to them was not in any way hoping for a hand-out; just communicating my tale of woe, nothing more, nothing less, like a shoulder to cry on. The outcome was a gift by the insurers offering a retrospective award. It was absolutely amazing and as far as I was concerned, something unheard of and a blessing indeed. A decision was taken not to reinstate the two cabins but just the one to house the community shop and locate it in front of the church buildings where it would be seen from the road and its visual presence would discourage foul play. A good sizeable second-hand cabin was purchased, craned up and over the wall onto its new location and in no time at all, the shop was open again and even boasted a fitting room or rather, cubicle.

St. Andrew's Roof Stolen

Claims to Methodist Insurance were an all too frequent occurrence due to break-ins; broken windows and smashed up internal doors. An infamous theft at St. Andrew's clearly left its mark! A call first thing in the morning from someone in the Shell administrative block housed behind the church asked if we knew there was a big hole in the church roof. On close inspection, the theft of three quarters of the copper from one side of the roof was without doubt carried out by professionals, something the police endorsed. Emergency measures included tarpaulin being wrapped all over the open space while conversations ensued with the insurers. "Did you realise" said the voice at the other end, "there is a clause in your insurance that the theft of metal will only have minimum cover and copper is a metal isn't it?" And a miniscule amount it was compared with the size of the overall bill for the roof but, worse was to follow. Difficult as it was on such a high roof for the tarpaulin to be effective against the elements, the inevitable happened! The church was awash with rain water and the wooden parquet floor wrecked, in fact in no time at all the whole interior needed to be redecorated besides a completely new parquet floor installed. No wonder I was heard to say on a few occasions that the grand piano in church was of more value as an insured item than the roof. Give Methodist Insurance the credit they deserve because we did negotiate a very acceptable figure towards a new roof as well as paying out for a complete new wooden parquet floor and complete redecoration. Sometimes the work of the Kingdom of God can seem solitary and full of problems and setbacks and then out of the blue, you realise there is help and support and you're not as much on your own as you thought.

Banging your head against a brick wall

The experience of banging your head against a brick wall, speaking metaphorically about officials in the Methodist Church, was all too common. Such occurrences always raised a host of questions to which it seemed there were too few answers. On the one hand what we were doing 'outside the box' was probably perceived by officials as being too unconventional and too risky with not enough control over our free-spirited idiosyncrasies; in other words, being just too radical. On the other hand working outside the box meant we were living out the Kingdom of God and at the same time we were being true to our Methodist history and heritage.

What follows are a few examples of this dichotomy with the Methodist Church represented through its administrative structures, personnel and committees hidebound on procedure and precedence over consideration and aspiration.

Legal Issues and Solicitors

Having so many partner organisations leasing our churches, Methodist Trust property as our buildings were, required credible professional legal advice and the means to process the necessary leasing and licensing contracts of the buildings or their various parts. Sometimes this required the use of an architect and surveyor especially in the redesigning of rooms and upgrading the premises to the point of major transformations. Professional services always meant a significant financial outlay, so funds would be needed and in place even at the initial stages of the enterprises. In addition to this the bureaucratic red tape with the property and legal authorities of the church, all too often seemed like an administrative burden or more accurately, an albatross. This is illustrated very well when advice was sought from the Church's Legal personnel concerning the services of a solicitor. Following a strong lead from them for a good solicitor, a local Methodist living in the Manchester area and fitting all the required qualities and experience was recommended. Having agreed to represent the Churches and our Methodist Circuit, one of the leases to be written up and adopted, was with an organisation which had already proved their worth as a partner organisation, and were proposing to make a substantial long term investment in the church they were leasing. It needs to be noted that their investment was a refurbishment scheme consisting of a large proportion of the premises at a cost to themselves of £50,000.

After a lengthy period with seemingly no progress towards an acceptable contract around which a lease could be agreed and signs of an impending bitter dispute, our church's carefully chosen solicitor began saying we could sue our partner organisation for being uncooperative and wasting time. It was obvious to me that if anyone was at fault it was our solicitor and if I left him to pursue matters in the way he was, we would simply go round in circles with ever more ill-judged recriminations. I made it clear to the solicitor that I had had enough and would organise a get-together for both parties around a table at which we would stay until we agreed on the contract. That seemed to do the trick. The process speeded up significantly and in no time at all we were signing and sealing the deal. In a conversation with the Methodist legal personnel, I asked why they had recommended this particular solicitor but alas, no satisfactory answer was forthcoming.

This difficulty refers to the withdrawal by the housing association in the quest to build a residential home for elderly people in the name of Healthy Living Network, at Baguley Hall's church's Harvest Centre featured in chapter 4. The housing association was the Manchester Methodist Housing Association and was regarded by the Manchester and Stockport Methodist District as a Methodist organisation.

Methodist Districts are large geographical areas not dissimilar to dioceses, and they incorporate ministers and lay people representing all the churches in the district at meetings called Synods. The synods are designed to be a resource to the churches which includes: training, leadership, support as well as governance and pastoral oversight. As a respected housing association with a long established partnership with the Methodist Church, I took the opportunity to appraise our District Synod on the way the housing association without warning and at the eleventh hour, withdrew their involvement in the project. No clear reasons were given. The interest they had shown simply vanished, and this was after extensive and detailed research conducted by Methodist Homes as part of a feasibility study.

In my address to synod, I appealed for support and understanding for our beleaguered people and asked for clarity over the housing association's status as a Methodist organisation. My thinking was that if part of the housing association's brief included a form of Methodist missiology (Methodist work and/or mission), synod might be able to act as go-between or even as a pressure group for our Baguley Hall church and Methodist Homes. There was no discussion, no questions, no feedback, just a feeling of isolation and the distinct impression that I was wrong to be questioning the validity of the housing association, and the way I was challenging its conduct. Hence the silence from the assembled gathering and a decision that the matter be put on the agenda of a synod sub-committee.

Apart from some sympathy from a few fellow ministers, I heard nothing more, not even whether the subject was mentioned when the sub-committee may have eventually held its meeting. At the very least it would have been helpful if the relationship between the Manchester Methodist Housing Association and Synod had been clarified and the extent to which, if any, the latter could influence the former. In the event, the vocational approach to the mission of our five churches was in stark contrast to the apparent indifference of the Methodist Manchester and Stockport District and its officers. The outcome left me feeling abandoned by Methodist brethren with whom I have always wanted to believe and feel I had a strong spiritual bond, and a Methodist gathering that failed to live up to the calling it claims to cherish.

Another controversial issue, this time with the Manchester and Stockport Methodist District was over the submission of annual church membership figures. Every year Methodist Circuits submit an audit of church members listing those who have died, moved away, ceased to be members, new members etc. Operating as we were on a housing estate with such heterogeneous and cosmopolitan communities, together with the professional and voluntary organisations and their leaders/managers, meant we were increasingly one body of people. Separating people between church members and non-church members, between those with whom we had strong ties for one reason or another from those who were 'signed up' religious and approved, was to differentiate between people and categorise them. The statistical returns required of me at that time, was something I simply could not and refused to do. To have complied with such a regulation would have been to drive a wedge between people, all of whom were playing their part in the work of the Kingdom of God. In consequence, when the membership figures were published each year, the sum total of our Wythenshawe churches was registered as nil returns. The forms changed slightly and began to include 'others' in the various categories, I was persuaded to try and make the best of a poor job, and did so very reluctantly, because the whole approach still smacked of a 'them' and 'us' approach.

We found a way to resolve this dilemma one Sunday when members of all five church congregations came together for a combined service. On those occasions more than usual people from the projects were likely to be in attendance. I decided to use the occasion to present annual church membership tickets. Among the congregation were those 'signed up' members for whom tickets were customarily issued. Also present were the 'unsigned up' members but who were just as much part of the church scene and work of the Kingdom as anyone else. As part of my sermon and with some explanation, I invited anyone in the congregation who wished to acknowledge their own sense of belonging, to collect from a pile of membership tickets one for themselves, write their name on it and present it to me for my signature. After the service there was quite a queue of people with their tickets, upon which they had written their names!

These scenarios including the housing association featured in chapter 4 under Healthy Living Network, illustrate the on-going dilemma I and we as a circuit had with Methodist officialdom and the frustration with a Church denomination that fails to accommodate a practical living theology of the Kingdom of God. There were many more similar scenarios that discriminated between people and their circumstances and chief among them was the populace being 'working-class'.

It seemed inevitable when I began my ministry in Wythenshawe that if the five churches continued operating in the traditional way expected of them by the Methodist Church, they would very quickly fall apart as church communities and close down. Like many institutions the Methodist Church assumes its lay people are experienced in professional administration, have a rounded education, are self-confident, articulate, used to systems and time management and last but not least, have experience in and enjoy participating in committees. It is precisely those roles that were not the strengths of the majority of working class people keen to play a pro-active part in the life of the church. The Methodist Church, on the whole has failed miserably to devise a structure of administration to be inclusive of all backgrounds. Furthermore, the literature and material published by the Church did not allow for a readership from a working class background and worse was the middleclass-ness of church meetings, committees, synods and the like. It was for these reasons that I with my administrative team took over so much of the church administration and at the same time developed a different structure to run all the church and project work efficiently and in a professional way as detailed in chapter 2 headed: 'Getting organised and the Acts of the Apostles'. Officialdom in the Methodist Church at all levels showed their disapproval at this different form of management, but what was most important was the smooth running of everything, with as many lay people as possible, having good governance and operating as one team with both church and partner organisations. All of that was achieved and proved to be successful.

A further issue that would have caused consternation if the church authorities had known about it, was over the authorisation of a lay person to preside at services of Holy Communion. It is standard procedure in certain circumstances for a lay person, usually someone who is an accredited local preacher, to do everything in a communion service that an ordained minister would do. This applies especially to churches where there are too few ministers with too many churches and rely on the services of local preachers. The way it is judged appropriate for a lay person to be authorised is by counting the number of actual church members and if the number reaches a certain numerical sum, authorisation to a lay person is granted. Having added up the actual church members of all five churches, it was considered by the church authorities that a lay person wasn't required to conduct communion services, despite myself at that time being the only full-time Methodist minister for the five churches. In order to rectify the situation and make communion services more available, I took it upon myself to authorise someone without any official permission or approval. I did this without anyone knowing except the person concerned by writing a statement of authorisation myself and made it applicable to the person I judged to be qualified. The calibre expected of someone was in the gifts and graces that were noticeable in the local preacher appointed for the role. As well as being held in high regard by the congregations, she was well read in liturgy and theology and experienced in pastoral care. Thus her 'priestly' role was accepted by the people, a role which she exercised with the dignity and reverence anyone would expect.

It is interesting that when the Church operates automatically in an institutional way, its roots that it claims to revere and continues to live out, are obscured. The Methodist Church emerged as a non-conformist movement and developed a distinctive appeal by doing things unconventionally. Within that fusion of spirit-led endeavour and social interaction was a missionary zeal characterised by the same signs of the Kingdom of God as were prominent in our pioneering or rather, revolutionary work. Revolution is what Christ was inaugurating through his Kingdom of God ministry and parabolic teaching, a revolution that became our revolution; a vision of society that became our vision and an unconventional style that became our style. Sadly for us, it attracted the all too familiar ways institutions bear down on such so called revolutionary working practices, just as they did in Christ's day.

Tension between institutional officialdom and our adopted Wythenshawe methodology is, on the one hand understandable and it explains the theological imperatives that were the essence of our work. On the other hand, it demonstrates our wish also to be true to our Methodist heritage, and at the same time shape our ministry to meet the needs of local contextualised mission and service.

There is a common thread here with the writings of liberation theologians like Leonardo Boff, Jon Sobrino, Gustavo Gutierrez and others. Their context was the gross poverty, oppression and injustice among communities in and around Latin America and the failure of church and state to do anything about it. As the title suggests, liberation theology addresses the peoples' situation by interpreting Christ's teaching in ways which liberates the people at the same time as giving them the stature and prominence they should have by right.

Commenting on Christ's pro-activeness, Jon Sobrino says this: Christ's actions are not simply accompaniments to his words, nor are they primarily designed to illustrate his own person. Their primary value is theo-logical. They are meant to demonstrate the Kingdom of God. The coming of the Kingdom means to Jesus, that the Kingdom is the transformation of a bad situation, of an oppressive situation, and that God's activity can only be envisioned as the overcoming of a negative situation." "Thus Jesus' whole activity, including his miracles and his pardoning of sins, must be viewed primarily in terms of the Kingdom of God drawing near to liberate people."

And personal liberation was at the forefront of their message, a liberation created not just from the poverty, oppression and injustice all around them shocking as that was, but by the ineptitude of the church and the corruption of the state to do anything about it. That familiar scenario occurs precisely when the true vision and dynamic is lost and everything becomes institutional.

Pushing the Kingdom of God boundaries out further, Gutierrez reinforces the universality of the Kingdom and goes even further, by saying its authority and influence expands into the social and political arena as well. "This is the Kingdom of God Jesus reveals to us in his de facto practice - a messianic practice, a practice that turns topsy-turvy not only our values, but historical realities and social status as well." Interpreting Kingdom of God as God's love revealed to the poor, Gutierrez makes a further observation, that the poor are the ones who receive, understand, and proclaim this love. In other words, the poor in relation to the Kingdom of God fulfils a prophetic role in that, as well as being recipients of God's love, at the same time they proclaim God's Kingdom.

WAYS & MEANS

There was no one way of finding potential organisations to form rock solid working relationships, but having made one or two working relationships and with the message already being out there, the majority of organisations came to us. Having decided upon the main area of service-led work to be pioneered and then wording it in the form of mission statements, each of the churches' small sub groups of two or three people sent the message out to organisations and personnel involved in community development, social cohesion and social regeneration. Sending the message out meant looking up organisations that were already pro-active in the area of work the churches had designated to do and then contact was made with them. Many of the organisations in turn referred us to others as well as sharing the message to an even wider network of people, groups and organisations.

Another form of 'message sending' was by conducting a questionnaire and taking it around to anyone and everyone; it was filled in with the answers from people and organisations, we were automatically giving out valuable details and information about our proposed schemes of work. I remember doing this in the name of 'New Dawn' and standing outside primary schools nabbing the parents while they were waiting for their children. Other locations visited with the questionnaire were health centres, doctors' surgeries, schools, leisure and day centres, housing associations, local councillors, local citizens advice centres besides others. I remember doing a feasibility study on specialised tracking equipment for people with acute needs which took me to a number of centres that specialised in that area of work and by so doing, our message was being passed around an even wider network of organisations.

Some organisations got in touch like the South Manchester Mental Health and Social Care Trust from which was born New Horizons Studio One. Southside Speech and Drama Group was similarly inspired. New Dawn's Counselling emerged from a conversation in my living room initiated by someone qualified in counselling, the person in question had 'an idea' about a counselling service and shared it with me. Likewise with New Dawn's alternative therapies, a professional physiotherapist from a neighbouring Methodist church got in touch after a service at her church where mention was made of our Wythenshawe work. Being the venue for and inviting all community orientated groups, organisations and personnel to a forum where ideas were shared and exchanged, was another way of getting the message out there and across a swathe of the estate and as a public relations exercise it more than proved its worth.

Among the first 'settlers' creating a partnership with the churches were two After School Clubs and because they were regulated by government legislation, essential alterations in the name of health and safety to the premises were necessary and that initiated, what became for all the churches, programmes of major refurbishment. The gym at Brownley Green was already up and running before we embarked upon our new mission of enterprises as was the rummage in the name of New Dawn plus a few other activities. I think they fulfilled the role of 'prophet' as they heralded a new age, a new style of service-led ministry before the Kingdom of God concept had well and truly become the cornerstone of our work.

FREQUENTLY ASKED QUESTIONS

Who were the partner organisations?

Over the period of the fifteen years and spread out over the five churches including St. Andrew's House, there were thirty-six partner organisations in all. Too many to list but all of them from the largest organisation to the smallest group were equally cherished.

How difficult was it to link up with appropriate partners?

As the message got out about our vision and determination to make it a reality, it was not difficult to find and team up with the different organisations and community groups. What was essential was the commitment of the statutory organisations because of the long-term investment of their specialised work and the rental that accrued.

What staff was employed by the projects?

At different intervals, WO employed four project managers besides periods when the project management was overseen by the chairperson. The statutory organisations employed their own managers and staff, whilst other organisations and voluntary groups were overseen by their own leaders.

How were the initial surveys instigated?

We used church members' knowledge concerning the needs of their local communities and neighbourhoods; and then in some instances drawing up questionnaires and in others button-holing personnel from selected organisations and groups. Some 'surveys' were part and parcel of formal and informal conversations with a wide range of community practitioners, collating and examining the information, which was then used to pilot the projects and be a source of information for funding applications.

How did church members feel about non church members being part of everything?

Having accepted the plan of action derived from the first detailed Plan submitted in January 1999, acknowledging the need for and future value of representatives from partner organisations seemed instinctive. Relationships between church and organisations were helped immeasurably by all sitting together and being equal members of the churches project management teams, added to which there were always occasions when church and non-church people would be mixing and mingling together. Appreciating the overall theological principle being voiced and acted upon was the Kingdom of God; it is not surprising that message went a long way in drawing church and non-church people together.

What is the present situation?

In 2012 the Wythenshawe Methodist Circuit (group of 5 churches) teamed up with its neighbouring Bramhall Circuit of 8 churches to form the Bramhall and Wythenshawe Circuit and in 2013 I moved out of Wythenshawe into retirement. Everything was operating more or less as before at that time. I do not have information, reports and general low-down to offer a sufficient up to date critique of the present situation.

EPILOGUE

In this book I have tried to reveal some of the very important and significant truths I have discovered in my ministry in Wythenshawe.

The truth about people especially, those from a working class background, and the work of God within the setting of working class culture;

The truth about exercising such a ministry and work outside the box, not because it is fashionable, but because it is essential, a necessity;

The truth about the pitfalls and difficulties such a diverse and non-traditional ministry creates, not least with its church hierarchy represented through its institution;

The truth about ordinary people shamefully side-lined by society and the wider church but who possess a spiritual side to their lives that exhibit images of the unseen Christ;

The truth about the Incarnate God and the coming of Christ over and over again in the disguise of those who might be considered least in his Kingdom;

The truth about finding the most appropriate model for contemporary church work and ministry and using it as a template and as on-going interpretation of biblical insights and truths;

The truth about working in partnership with non-church organisations, appreciating the integrity of their philosophical approach and capitalising on the complementary benefit to themselves and to the churches;

The truth about all people, without distinction, being assured their place in the family of God which by its integral nature invalidates man-made systems of membership as applied by the churches;

The truth about the Kingdom of God and the way modern church projects are parables in their own right and can be appropriately aligned to their biblical counterparts;

The truth about knowing when it is right to take risks as a proper exercise of faith, being a faithful pastor, leader, co-worker and fellow pilgrim with the people;

The truth about taking stock, listening to the people, being honest and being professional;

The truth about drawing up plans, following the plans through, retaining the vision, working as a team and building it all on the foundation of the Kingdom of God;

The truth about five Methodist church communities who could easily have been expected to react emotionally and nostalgically about their church's past glories, with the wish to retain the status quo and not attempt a radical future. But who in the midst of the biggest changes their premises had ever seen, like giving over of valued church space, their resounding response was more than simply resignation to the inevitable. It was full of courteousness, good grace and a hope that all the new futures will be successful. Like a remnant of previous generations, they had clearly become a Kingdom people for future generations.

And finally, the truth behind some of the most prophetic words spoken by Christ; prophetic in his day and realised prophecy in ours. In fact it is that realised prophecy which resonates throughout the whole of this story, right through to the liberating truth it exposes. The truth that the humble and poor, the sincere and the generous, the hard workers and those who never give up, the faithful and the faithless, the inspired and the receptive listener, the low self-esteem and the encourager; it is these people through whom Christ has chosen to walk the streets again.

GLOSSARY

Agape: Selfless sacrificial love

Beatitudes: Matthew 5:3-12

Christlikeness: Revealing the demeanour and qualities of Christ

Circuit: A group of Methodist churches that work collaboratively and operate administratively

Contextual: Appertaining to the here and now or relevant at the time of reference

Copperdale Trust: Provides a home for homeless young people and supports the work of the United Estates of Wythenshawe

Covenant Service: An annual service of personal re-dedication

Ecclesia: An assembly of Christian people

Ecclesiology: The nature and structure of the Christian Church

Emmaus Road: A resurrection appearance of Christ with two of his disciples in Luke 24:13-35

Gospel: The good news of Christ as told by the four gospel writers

Holistic: Wholeness; all the parts are interconnected

Incarnate God: God in human form

Incarnation: The presence of the divine within creation and humanity

Last Supper: The meal Jesus shared with his disciples at the time of the Passover

Liturgy: An act of worship with recognisable components

Magnificat: The Song of Mary the mother of Jesus in Luke 1: 46-55

Messianic: Appreciation of Jesus Christ as being the Messiah

Ministry; Ministries: The day-to-day work of Jesus and the day-to-day project work of the churches

OfQual: The Office of Qualifications and Examinations Regulation

Parabolic: Appertaining to the stories told by Jesus

P.R.: Personal relationships

Questionnaires: The Wythenshawe Questionnaire used for evaluation and assessment is held on file with Rev. David Bown

Sermon on the Mount: A range of Christ's teaching in Matthew 5-7

Social Cohesion: People in society who come together for good relationships and harmony

Social and Spiritual Regeneration: Renewal of life and energy in society and in people's spiritual lives

Spiritual: The essence of something or someone that is not material or physical

Synoptic Gospels: The books of Matthew, Mark and Luke

Theology: Redefining the God of the Bible for contemporary times; a study of the nature and being of God

Transfiguration: A spiritual transformation as in Matthew 17:1-8 & Mark 9:2-8

U.C.A.S.: Universities and Colleges Admissions Service

Whit Walks: Religious parades in commemoration and celebration of Pentecost

Wythenshawe Oasis (W.O.): The charity established by Wythenshawe Methodist Circuit

BIBLIOGRAPHY

Elliott, Charles. **Praying the Kingdom**
Darton Longman and Todd London 1985

Gutierrez, Gustavo. **The Power of the Poor in History**
SCM Press 1983

Hill, David. **The Gospel of Matthew**
New Century Bible Commentary Series 1972

Mother Teresa. **Love until it Hurts**
Harpercollins 1981

Nolan, Albert. **Jesus before Christianity**
Darton Longman and Todd London 1992

Richardson, Alan. **A Dictionary of Christian Theology**
SCM Press 1969

Sobrino, Jon. **Christology at the Crossroads**
SCM Press 1978

Tillich, Paul. **The Shaking of the Foundations**
Pelican Books 1962

Ward, J. Neville. **Beyond Tomorrow**
Epworth Press1981

Wesley, Charles. From the hymn: **O for a thousand tongues to sing**

BIBLICAL REFERENCES

Preface:

- Luke 1:52-53.
- Matthew 5:1-7., 5:1-12., 9:35-38.,11:4-5., 25:40.
- Mark 15:43.
- John 1:11.

Chapter 2:

- Luke 7:1-10.
- Acts chapters 2 & 4.

Chapter 3:

- Luke 7:1-10.
- Matthew 13:33., 20:1.
- Mark 12:34.

Chapter 4:

- Luke 10:25-35., 14:15-24., 15:11-31.
- John 6:1-13.
- Mark 10:13-16.
- Ephesians 5:30.
- Matthew 25:31-46.
- Acts 2:42-47.

Chapter 5

- Luke 18:16-17.
- Matthew 7:7-8.
- Luke 7:1-10.

Chapter 6

- Luke 14:15-23.

Chapter 7

- Acts 8:26-40.
- Isaiah 53:1-12.
- Luke 10:38-42., 17:12-19., 19:1-10.
- Mark 7:24-30.